First World War
and Army of Occupation
War Diary
France, Belgium and Germany

8 DIVISION
24 Infantry Brigade
Worcestershire Regiment
1st Battalion
16 October 1914 - 29 March 1919

WO95/1723/1

The Naval & Military Press Ltd
www.nmarchive.com
Published in association with The National Archives

Published by

The Naval & Military Press Ltd

Unit 10 Ridgewood Industrial Park,

Uckfield, East Sussex,

TN22 5QE England

Tel: +44 (0) 1825 749494

www.naval-military-press.com

www.nmarchive.com

This diary has been reprinted in facsimile from the original. Any imperfections are inevitably reproduced and the quality may fall short of modern type and cartographic standards.

© **Crown Copyright**
Images reproduced by permission of The National Archives, London, England, 2015.

Contents

Document type	Place/Title	Date From	Date To
Heading	8th Division 24th Infy Bde 1st Bn Worcestershire Regt Oct 1914-Apl 1919		
Miscellaneous	DAG GHQ 3rd Echelon	02/09/1918	02/09/1918
Heading	23rd Division 24th Infy Bde 1st Bn Worcs Regt Nov 1915-Jun 1916		
Heading	8th Division 24th Inf. Bde War Diary 1st Worcestershire 16-31 October November 1914		
War Diary	Liverpool	16/10/1914	17/10/1914
War Diary	Winchester	17/10/1914	05/11/1914
War Diary	Southampton	05/11/1914	05/11/1914
War Diary	Havre	08/11/1914	09/11/1914
War Diary	Abbeville	09/11/1914	09/11/1914
War Diary	Berguette	10/11/1914	11/11/1914
War Diary	Neuf Berquin	11/11/1914	14/11/1914
War Diary	St Vaast	14/11/1914	14/11/1914
War Diary	A Lines	14/11/1914	19/11/1914
War Diary	La Gorgue	19/11/1914	21/11/1914
War Diary	A Lines	22/11/1914	24/11/1914
War Diary	Pont Du Hem	25/11/1914	25/11/1914
War Diary	Red Barn	25/11/1914	27/11/1914
War Diary	A Lines	28/11/1914	01/12/1914
Miscellaneous	1st Bn Worcestershire Regiment	05/11/1914	05/11/1914
Map	Map		
Diagram etc	Diagram		
Heading	8th Division 24th Inf Bde War Diary 1st Worcestershire December 1914		
War Diary		02/12/1914	04/12/1914
War Diary	A Lines	04/12/1914	07/12/1914
War Diary	Red Barn	07/12/1914	10/12/1914
War Diary	A Lines	10/12/1914	18/12/1914
War Diary	B Lines	19/12/1914	22/12/1914
War Diary	La Gorgue	22/12/1914	25/12/1914
War Diary	B Lines	25/12/1914	28/12/1914
War Diary	Red Barn	29/12/1914	31/12/1914
Diagram etc	Archibald		
Map	Map		
Heading	8th Division 1/Worcs Regt. Nov 1915 Vol XII		
War Diary		01/11/1914	30/11/1914
Heading	8th Division 24th Brigade 1st Worcesters January 1915		
Heading	24th Brigade 1st Worcesters Vol III 1-31.1.15		
War Diary	B Lines	01/01/1915	03/01/1915
War Diary	La Gorgue	04/01/1915	06/01/1915
War Diary	B Lines	07/01/1915	09/01/1915
War Diary	Red Barn	09/01/1915	11/01/1915
War Diary	B Lines	11/01/1915	27/01/1915
War Diary	La Gorgue	28/01/1915	30/01/1915
War Diary	B Lines	31/01/1915	31/01/1915
Miscellaneous	1st Bn Worcestershire Regiment	01/01/1915	01/01/1915
Miscellaneous	Orders To Lieut Roberts By Major E67 Wodehouse D.S.O.	03/01/1915	03/01/1915

Type	Description	Start	End
Miscellaneous	Orders To Artillery Observation Officer By Major E67 Wodehouse D.S.O. 1st Bn Worcestershire Regt	03/01/1915	03/01/1915
Miscellaneous	Instructions Given by Lieut F.C Roberts Ware Regt to his Party		
Heading	8th Division 24th Brigade 1st, Worcester Regt February 1915		
Heading	24th Brigade 1st Worcester Vol IV 1-28.2.15		
War Diary	B Lines	01/02/1915	08/02/1915
War Diary	La Gorgue	09/02/1915	11/02/1915
War Diary	B Lines	11/02/1915	14/02/1915
War Diary	Red Barn	15/02/1915	17/02/1915
War Diary	B Lines	17/02/1915	20/02/1915
War Diary	La Gorgue	21/02/1915	23/02/1915
War Diary	B Lines	23/02/1915	26/02/1915
War Diary	Red Barn	26/02/1915	28/02/1915
Heading	8th Division 24th Brigade 1st Worcester Regt. March 1915		
Heading	24th Brigade 1st Worcesters Vol V 1.3-3.4.15		
War Diary	Red Barn	01/03/1915	01/03/1915
War Diary	B Lines	01/03/1915	04/04/1915
Miscellaneous	8 Div BM.296	27/03/1915	27/03/1915
Miscellaneous	Extract From War Diary 1st Bn Worcestershire Regt On Operations From The 9th-13th March 1915	13/03/1915	13/03/1915
Heading	8th Division 24th Brigade 1st Worcester Regt. April/May 1915		
Heading	8th Division 1st Worcesters Vol VI 5.4-31.5.15		
War Diary		05/04/1915	31/05/1915
Heading	8th Division 24th Brigade 1st Worcester Regt June 1915		
Heading	8th Division 1st Worcesters Vol VII 1-30.6.15		
War Diary		01/06/1915	30/06/1915
Heading	8th Division 24th Brigade 1st Worcester Regt July 1915		
Heading	8th Division 1st Worcesters Vol VIII 1-31.7.15		
War Diary		13/07/1915	31/07/1915
Heading	8th Division 24th Brigade 1st Worcester Regt. August 1915		
Heading	8th Division 1st Worcesters Vol IX From 1-31.8.15		
War Diary		01/08/1915	31/08/1915
Heading	8th Division 24th Brigade 1st Worcester Regt. September 1915		
Heading	8th Division 1st Worcesters Vol X Sept 15		
War Diary		01/09/1915	30/09/1915
Heading	8th Division 24th Brigade 1st Worcester Regt October 1915		
Heading	8th Division 1st Worcesters Vol XI Oct 15		
War Diary		01/10/1915	31/10/1915
Miscellaneous	D.A.G Base	01/04/1917	01/04/1917
Heading	23rd Div 1/Worcesters Regt Dec Vol XIII		
War Diary		01/12/1915	31/12/1915
Heading	23rd Division 1st Bn Worcester Regt Jan Vol XIV		
War Diary		01/01/1916	30/04/1916
War Diary	Beaumetz	01/05/1916	05/05/1916
War Diary	Hersin	06/05/1916	10/05/1916
War Diary	Love HEZI	11/05/1916	15/05/1916
War Diary	Bouvigny	16/05/1916	20/05/1916
War Diary	Bouvigny Huts	21/05/1916	30/05/1916
War Diary	Angres II	31/05/1916	04/06/1916

War Diary	Fosse	05/06/1916	10/06/1916
War Diary	Angres II	11/06/1916	11/06/1916
War Diary	Fosse 10	12/06/1916	13/06/1916
War Diary	Dieval	13/06/1916	13/06/1916
War Diary	Fiefs	14/06/1916	15/06/1916
War Diary	Flechin	16/06/1916	24/06/1916
War Diary	St Sauveur	25/06/1916	30/06/1916
Heading	24th Inf. Bde. 8th Div. War Diary 1st Battn. The Worcestershire Regiment July 1916		
War Diary	Molliens Au Bois	01/07/1916	06/07/1916
War Diary	Fricourt	07/07/1916	10/07/1916
War Diary	Bresle	11/07/1916	11/07/1916
War Diary	Molliens Au Bois	12/07/1916	12/07/1916
War Diary	Pierrgot	13/07/1916	13/07/1916
War Diary	Poulainville	14/07/1916	14/07/1916
War Diary	Fouquereuil	15/07/1916	22/07/1916
War Diary	Beuvry	23/07/1916	31/07/1916
Heading	8th Division 24th Brigade 1st Worcester Regt August 1916		
War Diary	Cuinchy Trenches	01/08/1916	05/08/1916
War Diary	Billets	06/08/1916	09/08/1916
War Diary	Trenches	10/08/1916	15/08/1916
War Diary	Billets	16/08/1916	23/08/1916
War Diary	Trenches	24/08/1916	31/08/1916
Heading	8th Division 24th Brigade 1st Bn Worcester Regt September 1916		
War Diary	France	01/09/1916	01/09/1916
War Diary	Trenches	02/09/1916	09/09/1916
War Diary	Billets	10/09/1916	11/09/1916
War Diary	Labourse Billets	12/09/1916	17/09/1916
War Diary	Trenches	18/09/1916	30/09/1916
Heading	8th Division 24th Brigade 1st Bn Worcester Regt. October, 1916		
War Diary	France	01/10/1916	31/10/1916
Heading	8th Division 24th Brigade 1st Bn Worcester Regt. November 1916		
War Diary		01/11/1916	30/11/1916
Heading	8th Division 24th Brigade 1st Bn Worcester Regt. December 1916		
War Diary	Aumont	01/12/1916	31/12/1916
War Diary	In The Field	01/01/1917	28/02/1917
War Diary	Bray	01/03/1917	03/03/1917
War Diary	Bouchavesnes Trenches	04/03/1917	04/03/1917
War Diary	Asquith Flats	05/03/1917	07/03/1917
War Diary	Trenches	08/03/1917	31/03/1917
War Diary	Moislains	01/04/1917	08/04/1917
War Diary	Heudicourt	09/04/1917	16/04/1917
War Diary	Nurlu	17/04/1917	20/04/1917
War Diary	Guyencourt	21/04/1917	30/04/1917
War Diary	Trenches Between Villers Guislan & Honnecourt	01/05/1917	07/05/1917
War Diary	Vaucellette Farm	07/05/1917	15/05/1917
War Diary	Moislains	16/05/1917	31/05/1917
War Diary	Corbie	01/06/1917	28/06/1917
War Diary	Vancouver Camp	19/06/1917	30/06/1917
War Diary	Ypres	01/07/1917	05/07/1917
War Diary	Winnipeg Camp	06/07/1917	07/07/1917

War Diary	Steenbecque	08/07/1917	08/07/1917
War Diary	Cuhem	09/07/1917	18/07/1917
War Diary	Coyecque Area	19/07/1917	20/07/1917
War Diary	St Martin	21/07/1917	21/07/1917
War Diary	Reninghelst	22/07/1917	22/07/1917
War Diary	Halifax Camp	23/07/1917	23/07/1917
War Diary	Ypres	24/07/1917	26/07/1917
War Diary	Halfway House	27/07/1917	30/07/1917
War Diary	Near Hooge	30/07/1917	31/07/1917
War Diary	Hooge	31/07/1917	16/08/1917
War Diary	Ref Sheet Zille Beke	17/08/1917	19/08/1917
War Diary	Ref Sheet No.27	20/08/1917	23/08/1917
War Diary	Ref Sheet No.28 SW. SE	24/08/1917	31/08/1917
War Diary	Trenches	01/09/1917	31/12/1917
War Diary	Longuenesse	01/12/1917	25/12/1917
War Diary	Passchendaele	26/12/1917	31/12/1917
Miscellaneous	D.A.G 3rd Echelon Base	01/02/1918	01/02/1918
War Diary		01/01/1918	28/02/1918
Heading	24th Inf. Bde 8th Div. War Diary 1st Battn The Worcestershire Regiment March 1918		
War Diary		01/03/1918	31/03/1918
Miscellaneous	1st Battalion The Worcestershire Regiment Training Programme for The Period Monday 18th to Saturday 20th March 1918	20/03/1918	20/03/1918
Miscellaneous	Action Of The 1/Worcestershire Regt. Night 23rd/24th March 1918	10/08/1918	10/08/1918
Miscellaneous	H.Q. 2nd Rhine Brigade British Army of The Rhine.	24/05/1925	24/05/1925
Map	Map		
Heading	24th Brigade 8th Division 1st Battalion Worcestershire Regiment April 1918		
Miscellaneous	D.A.G 3rd Echelon Base	05/05/1918	05/05/1918
War Diary		01/04/1918	30/04/1918
Heading	D.A.G 3rd Echelon Base		
War Diary		01/05/1918	30/06/1918
Heading	D.A.G. GHQ 3rd Echelon		
War Diary	Dargnies	01/07/1918	04/07/1918
War Diary	Onival	05/07/1918	15/07/1918
War Diary	Dargnies	16/07/1918	20/07/1918
War Diary	Camblain L'abbe	21/07/1918	22/07/1918
War Diary	Petit Vimy	23/07/1918	30/07/1918
War Diary	Trenches	31/07/1918	26/08/1918
Heading	D.A.G. 3rd Echelon		
War Diary	Oppy Front	01/09/1918	30/09/1918
Miscellaneous	DAG GHQ	01/07/1918	01/07/1918
Heading	24th Bde. 8th Division War Diary 1st Bn Worcestershire Regt October 1918		
War Diary		01/10/1918	07/10/1918
War Diary	Under A T.M Barrage	07/10/1918	30/11/1918
Heading	D.A.G. 3rd Echelon		
War Diary		01/12/1918	28/02/1919
Miscellaneous	DAG 3rd Echelon	03/04/1919	03/04/1919
War Diary	ATH (Belgium)	01/03/1919	31/03/1919
War Diary	ATH	03/03/1919	29/03/1919

8TH DIVISION
24TH INFY BDE

1ST BN WORCESTERSHIRE REGT

OCT 1914 - APL 1919

(LESS NOV 1915 - JUN 1916)

DAAG GHQ
3rd Echelon

Herewith War Diary for
month of August 1918.

A. Shickim? H/ Lieut Colonel
Comdg 1st Bn The Worc Regt.

23RD DIVISION
24TH INFY BDE

1ST BN WORCS REGT.
NOV 1915 - JUN 1916

8th Division
24th Inf. Bde

Batta. disembarked
Havre from England
8.11.14

WAR DIARY

1st WORCESTERSHIRE

16-31 October &
November

1914

Army Form C. 2118

WAR DIARY
or
INTELLIGENCE SUMMARY.
(Erase heading not required.)

Instructions regarding War Diaries and Intelligence Summaries are contained in F.S. Regs., Part II. and the Staff Manual respectively. Title pages will be prepared in manuscript.

Hour, Date, Place		Summary of Events and Information	Remarks and References to Appendices
1914.			
Oct 16th LIVERPOOL	9.15pm	Battalion arrived on board H.M.T Devanha from ALEXANDRIA EGYPT and commenced to disembark. Trained families on board H.M.T CORSICAN disembarked and proceeded to their respective homes.	
Oct 17th LIVERPOOL	4.50am	Battalion less 6 officers and 4 platoons who were left to unload baggage entrained for WINCHESTER, train halted at BIRMINGHAM for ½ hour and troops were given hot coffee and sandwiches.	
Oct 17th WINCHESTER	3PM	arrived and marched to HORSLEY DOWN CAMP a distance of about 3½ miles. Battalion was dressed on serge clothing and kitbags on arrival and kitbags.	
"	4.15PM	Arrived + occupied Camp which had been pitched by the draft of Special and Army Reserves, and were awaiting our arrival.	
		The Battalion now formed part of the 24th Infantry Brigade under Br. Genl. 4 Carter and	

Army Form C. 2118.

WAR DIARY
or
INTELLIGENCE SUMMARY.
(Erase heading not required.)

Instructions regarding War Diaries and Intelligence Summaries are contained in F. S. Regs., Part II. and the Staff Manual respectively. Title pages will be prepared in manuscript.

Hour, Date, Place	Summary of Events and Information	Remarks and References to Appendices
October 17th to Nov 4th	The 8th Division under Maj. Genl. Frank Davies CB Battalion mobilised at HURSLEY. Every Officer and N C O and man was given 48 hours leave during this period.	
November 5th 12 Noon	Battalion marched from HORSLEY to SOUTHAMPTON	
Nov 5th SOUTHAMPTON 4 P.M.	DOCKS and embarked on H.M.T. MAIDAN.	Appendix I. List of Officers on this date. Strength 31 officers
11.45 P.M.	Sailed for HAVRE.	
Nov 8th HAVRE 9 am	Disembarked, remains unopened in the outer harbour for two days waiting for a berth. Billeted in a large iron hangar in the docks.	
Nov 9th HAVRE 5 P.M.	Entrained in one train for Railhead, actual destination only known by Commanding Officer.	
10th ABBEVILLE	Halted for ½ hour troops given coffee.	
10th BERGUETTE 6 P.M.	Detrained, Mr B Cochrane killed in error for duty, C.R.E. guide for R.E.s	
11th 10.30 am	Marched via MERVILLE to NEUF BERQUIN (2 miles)	

(9.29.6) W 2794 100,000 8/14 H W V Forms/C. 2118/11.

WAR DIARY
or
INTELLIGENCE SUMMARY.
(Erase heading not required.)

Army Form C. 2118

Hour, Date, Place	Summary of Events and Information	Remarks and References to Appendices
Nov 11th NEUF BERQUIN 2.30 PM	Billeted. Companies very much scattered.	
Nov 11th 12th 13th NEUF BERQUIN	Billets.	
Nov 14th NEUF BERQUIN 2.45 PM	Marched to ST VAAST via NEUF BERQUIN – ESTAIRES – ROUGE CROIX – CROIX BARBÉE	
3.45 PM	Halted ½ hour for tea, at PONT DE LA TROMPE. C.O. and O's C Companies rode on to H.d. Q.rs. A Line trenches to discuss relief with O.C. 1st Royal Scots, who we are relieving in the trenches.	
4 PM	Marched under Major Wordhouse and halted in mass 400x South of ST VAAST at 6 P.M., where ammunition up to 300 rounds per man was issued.	
ST VAAST 6.30 PM	Company Commanders returned to their Companies with Company guides from 1st ROYAL SCOTS.	
6.30 PM to 9 PM	Battalion relieved 1st ROYAL SCOTS in A Lines trenches. The relief was carried out by Companies, who filed in at the flank of the trench	

Army Form C. 2118

WAR DIARY
or
INTELLIGENCE SUMMARY.
(Erase heading not required.)

Hour, Date, Place	Summary of Events and Information	Remarks and References to Appendices

Nov 14th A LINES

Battalion relieves
2nd Royal Scots in A lines

and the Royal Scots moved out across country. Companies used two routes for the relief A & C Companies by Foresters Lane — B & D Coys by FORESTERS LANE then by LONG DITCH to point A, on sketch, then across the open to the trenches.

FORESTERS LANE was under incessant rifle fire both from the Germans in front of our lines, and from the Germans in front of the Indian lines, which run back at right angles along the RUE du BOIS. Sketch No 1 shows the disposition of Companies on this day. Sketch No 1 shows the general type of the trenches in A lines. The actual trench had been dug in the ditch running along the west side of the ESTAIRES – LA BASSEE road – Consequently the floor of the trench was very wet, also there was no rear parapet, and consequently

See Sketch No 1

WAR DIARY
or
INTELLIGENCE SUMMARY.
(Erase heading not required.)

Army Form C. 2118

Hour, Date, Place	Summary of Events and Information	Remarks and References to Appendices
Nov 14. ALINES continued.	as the trench was only about 4ft 6 to 5ft deep. Bullets from in front of the Indian lines were continually coming into the trenches, especially those of C & A Companies. At first it was thought that there were German snipers concealed in houses behind our lines.	
Description of Country.	The country in this neighbourhood is 62ft above sea level, and is exceedingly flat. Most of the fields are cultivated, and at this time are ploughed. ~~most of the fields which~~ vary very much in size, are surrounded by ditches, which apparently drain, or not as the case may be, into a number of larger drains, such as the long ditch. Most of these ditches have a row of willows on each side - there are also a certain number of hedges.	

WAR DIARY
or
INTELLIGENCE SUMMARY.
(Erase heading not required.)

Army Form C. 2118.

Hour, Date, Place	Summary of Events and Information	Remarks and References to Appendices
Nov 14. A.LINES continued.	The soil is almost everywhere a heavy reddish brown clay, with very few stones in it. The roads are narrow but well metalled, and are generally built up about 2ft above the country on each side, and in nearly every case there is a ditch on each side of the road. Signposts are plentiful and very clear.	
First night in trenches	This first night in the trenches was exceedingly trying to officers and men, as not having seen the country in daylight it was not even known how far the German trenches were in front of them or where the dispositions of the Regts on the flanks. It was difficult also to find, what communication trenches there were, and where they led to, and the positions of any support trenches in rear.	

Army Form C. 2118

WAR DIARY
or
INTELLIGENCE SUMMARY.
(Erase heading not required.)

Instructions regarding War Diaries and Intelligence Summaries are contained in F.S. Regs., Part II. and the Staff Manual respectively. Title pages will be prepared in manuscript.

Hour, Date, Place	Summary of Events and Information	Remarks and references to Appendices
November 14. A. Sinai.	The removal of wounded men was carried out under great difficulty. The system was roughly as follows:— Stretcher Bearers remained in the trenches with their Companies, during the day it was impossible to carry wounded back to the first aid post owing to rifle fire, consequently the wounded were bandaged as well as possible during the day, and waited in the trenches till dark. The Medical Officer (Lieut Gilchrist R.A.M.C.) frequently came down to the trenches in daylight to attend to serious cases. Owing to the trenches being extremely narrow a stretcher could not be used, so the wounded were helped along by the stretcher bearers as far as possible when they could be carried on stretchers to the 1st Aid Post. In certain cases they were carried the whole way across country.	
Disposal of Killed	Men who were killed remained in the trenches till dark and were then buried by their comrades in rear of the trench.	

WAR DIARY
or
INTELLIGENCE SUMMARY.
(Erase heading not required.)

Army Form C. 2118

Instructions regarding War Diaries and Intelligence Summaries are contained in F. S. Regs., Part II. and the Staff Manual respectively. Title pages will be prepared in manuscript.

Hour, Date, Place	Summary of Events and Information	Remarks and References to Appendices
Nov 14 A. LINES continued	Sentries were posted in two reliefs, one hour on and one hour off only. The manifested in his dugout. In A and C Companies the sentries in nearly every case lay on the top of the "dug outs" and was protected by headcover which however was by no means bulletproof. Sentries were always posted by night with fixed bayonets and full magazines.	
Position of Headquarters	Battalion Headquarters was situated in a farm 200 yards north of the junction of the RICHEBOURG ST VAAST Road and FORESTERS LANE. The Commanding Officer, Adjutant and Senior Major remained at headquarters with the headquarters Party consisting of the Support Major, Pioneer and Armourer Sergeants, signallers &c. The 1st Aid post was in a house 300° North	

WAR DIARY
or
INTELLIGENCE SUMMARY.
(Erase heading not required.)

Army Form C. 2118

Hour, Date, Place	Summary of Events and Information	Remarks and References to Appendices
Nov 14 H. LINES. continued	of Battalion Headquarters, where the Medical Officer and the Stretcher bearers lived at the 1st Aid Post. The Transport Officer and Quartermaster and the Transport remained at LA GORGUE whilst the Battalion was in the trenches.	
Rations	Marching into the trenches on the first night every man carried the next days rations, on the second night rations were brought up to Battalion Headquarters about 6 p.m. where the ration parties from each Company, consisting of the Company Quartermaster Sergeants and about 14 to 20 men per Company collected and carried the rations down to the trenches by hand. The ration parties each night had a very unpleasant job, as the roads & c. between the trenches and Headquarters were swept with bullets.	

Army Form C. 2118.

WAR DIARY
or
INTELLIGENCE SUMMARY.
(Erase heading not required.)

Instructions regarding War Diaries and Intelligence Summaries are contained in F. S. Regs., Part II. and the Staff Manual respectively. Title pages will be prepared in manuscript.

Hour, Date, Place	Summary of Events and Information	Remarks and References to Appendices
NOV 14 ALINES continued	The nights were generally very dark, the trenches very narrow and the loads heavy.	
	The daily rations were on a generous scale, and of excellent quality, each man getting per day, Bully Beef or fresh & vegetable ration Biscuits, tea, sugar, jam, Bacon and cheese. Cigarettes and matches were also provided every few days, together with "Comfort" funds.	
Fires	Fires were lit in the trenches so that they did not give light by night or smoke by day. Wood was procured from ruined houses behind the trenches, and there was also a small issue of coal and coke, which did not however go very far. The Officers in the trenches messed very much the same as the men, and in most cases	

(9 29 6) W 2794 103,000 8/14 H W V Forms/C. 2118/11.

WAR DIARY
or
INTELLIGENCE SUMMARY.
(Erase heading not required.)

Army Form C. 2118.

Hour, Date, Place	Summary of Events and Information	Remarks and References to Appendices
Nov 14 A LINES continued.	cooked their own meals, a few extras such as bread, eggs, pork chops &c were sent down from H.Q. mess. Headquarters dug out was also used as a depot for R.E. Stores which was carried by hand to the trenches. A reserve of at least 70,000 rounds S.A.A. was also kept at Headquarters, and sent down to the trenches as required. Battalion Headquarters was in telephonic communication with Headquarters 24th Infantry Brigade, and at intervals with 36th Battery R.F.A., who were supporting us. By day a Gunner officer in telephonic communication with his battery lived in the trenches. Lieut Dewar of 15th Company Royal Engineers frequently came round the trenches and assisted, in building "dug outs" laying out trenches &c.	

Army Form C. 2118

WAR DIARY
or
INTELLIGENCE SUMMARY.
(Erase heading not required.)

Instructions regarding War Diaries and Intelligence Summaries are contained in F. S. Regs., Part II. and the Staff Manual respectively. Title pages will be prepared in manuscript.

Hour, Date, Place	Summary of Events and Information	Remarks and References to Appendices
November 15th A Lines	A cold wind blowing from the North East, and rain most of the day.	
	At daylight it was possible to see the German trenches, which were about 60 yards in front of D Company, and about 250 yards in front of A Company and in the centre of the line the distance varied from 80 to 150 yards.	
	During the night incessant sniping was carried on by the Germans to which we did not reply, not being able to see any target.	
	There was also a good amount of sniping during the day by the Germans, both from their trenches and from houses in front of C Company, advanced trench.	
10.30 am	Germans commenced shelling behind 'C' Coys trenches with 5.9 High explosive shells, known as "Black Maria"	

(9-29-6) W 2754 103,000 8/14 H W V   Forms/C. 2118/11.

WAR DIARY
or
INTELLIGENCE SUMMARY.
(Erase heading not required.)

Army Form C. 2118.

Hour, Date, Place	Summary of Events and Information	Remarks and references to Appendices
11 am.	these however inflicted no casualties. They increased the range and found B Company in their support trench, pitching two shells actually in the trench, doing a good deal of damage to the trench and inflicting the following casualties Killed Wounded	
2 P.m.	Shelling ceased.	
5 P.m	B Company moved two platoons up into the fire trench between C and D Companies, and two platoons moved into the support trench behind the right of "C" Company. The night passed quietly except for about half an hour between 9 and 10 when the Regt on our left (2nd Northamptons) commenced rapid fire, which was taken up by our men, and was difficult to stop. A few Germans apparently came out of their trenches	Casualties up to midnight 14/15 7 killed Lt Leman & 24 O.R. wounded
November 16th		

Army Form C. 2118/4

WAR DIARY
or
INTELLIGENCE SUMMARY.
(*Erase heading not required.*)

Instructions regarding War Diaries and Intelligence Summaries are contained in F.S. Regs., Part II. and the Staff Manual respectively. Title pages will be prepared in manuscript.

Hour, Date, Place	Summary of Events and Information	Remarks and references to Appendices
Nov 16	Opposite D Company who accounted for 3 or 4 of them.	
8 am to Noon	Germans ranged with 5.9" on support trench occupied by 2 platoons B Company, no damage done, shells dropping over and short of trench.	
10 PM 2 am	Communication trench started by B Company between long ditch and D Company's trenches	Casualties to M.N 2 killed 1 wounded
Nov 17th	Extremely cold and a while frost during the night, causing trouble to the men put which were still wet from previous rain.	
November 17th Notts Ft	Germans opened fire with same guns as yesterday on B Companies support trench and put 4 shells into the trench, and continued shelling for about an hour, only killing one man.	
8.15 am	Trench evacuated - platoons moving into ditch on east side of road and in front of C Company	

(9 29 6) W 2794 100,000 8/14 H W V   Forms/C. 2118/11.

Army Form C. 2118.

15

WAR DIARY
or
INTELLIGENCE SUMMARY.
(Erase heading not required.)

Hour, Date, Place	Summary of Events and Information	Remarks and references to Appendices
Nov 17th 2 P.m. 6 a.m.	Germans shelled left of line and dropped 6 shells into trench occupied by machine gun, but inflicted no casualties, as the trench had been evacuated.	
3 P.m.	Several farms in rear of our trenches were shelled	Casualties 6 n.n. 1 Killed 6 wounded
Nov. 18th A.m.	Germans still shelling behind our lines, inflicting however few casualties	
2 P.m. 4 P.m.	The two platoons of B Coy on East of Road shelled three shells pitching in trench inflicting following casualties 2 killed Sergt Heaslehead of wounds	
5 P.m.	ditch on west of road in continuation of C Company's right and behind other two platoons of B Company	

Army Form C. 2118
16

WAR DIARY
or
INTELLIGENCE SUMMARY.
(Erase heading not required.)

Instructions regarding War Diaries and Intelligence Summaries are contained in F.S. Regs., Part II. and the Staff Manual respectively. Title pages will be prepared in manuscript.

Hour, Date, Place	Summary of Events and Information	Remarks and references to Appendices
Nov 19th.	Snowed last night, country white, the first time some of our men from India had seen snow for 8 or 9 years. The day passed quietly.	Casualties to M.N. 6 killed 17 wounded.
7 P.M.	Battalion was relieved by 2nd Battn Sherwood Foresters. Relief was carried out by Platoons who assembled in a field behind headquarters, where they had to wait for about an hour, for the Battalion to collect. This perhaps was the most trying hour of the spell in the trenches, the ground was covered with snow, a cold north east wind was blowing - with 17° of frost. Officers and men's clothes were wet and the whole Battalion dead tired.	Casualties during 19th 4 killed. 3 Wounded.
8 P.M.	Battalion moved off to Billets at LA GORGUE. This march over a distance of 6 miles is	Total casualties during 5 days in trenches. Killed . 20 Wounded 1 Officer 51 O.R.

17

Army Form C. 2118

WAR DIARY
or
INTELLIGENCE SUMMARY.
(Erase heading not required.)

Hour, Date, Place	Summary of Events and Information	Remarks and references to Appendices
LA GORGUE Nov 19th	known as the "Retreat from Moscow". Mens feet were frost bitten and sore, the roads slippery and equipment and clothing soaked, consequently rate of march was only about 1½ miles per hour. Nevertheless by some means or other the whole Battalion arrived at LA GORGUE at 2-30 A.m where it billeted and formed part of Divisional Reserve. February 8th 1915 Stockhouse Major Cmdg 1st Worcestershire Regiment.	

WAR DIARY or INTELLIGENCE SUMMARY.

Army Form C. 2118.

1st Worcestershire Regt

Hour, Date, Place	Summary of Events and Information	Remarks and References to Appendices
1914.		
LA GORGUE Nov 20th	Billets. 1 Officer (Capt C.H.G. CRAWFORD) 146 men admitted to hospital with sore and frostbitten feet.	
11 P.M.	Germans put about 12, 5.9 howitzer shells into Sheffield road to our transport, but no casualties.	NOV 21st Lieut. R.M. SLATER wounded bullet back of head - died of wounds in hospital, buried in MERVILLE
LAGORDE Nov 21st A Lines November 22	Relieved 2nd Sherwood Foresters in A Lines.	Strength 21 Officers in trenches 625 O.R.
23	Trenches beginning to get very muddy, owing to rain, but having been dug deeper, afforded better cover, which explains the smaller number of casualties.	Casualties during Nov 22, 23, 24, 25 3 Killed 5 Wounded.
		NOV 22nd 1st Reinforcement - 40 Rank & file.
PONT DU HEM November 25	Marched out of trenches at dusk and marched by Companies to billets at Pont du Hem, known as "RED BARN".	
	When occupying billets at RED BARN The Battalion is in Brigade Reserve, and two companies are always in a state of readiness to turn out at very short notice	

Army Form C. 2118.
18

WAR DIARY
or
INTELLIGENCE SUMMARY.
(Erase heading not required.)

Hour, Date, Place	Summary of Events and Information	Remarks and References to Appendices
November 25th RED BARN	These Companies change every day, at 6 P.M. The Battalion stands to arms at dawn, and for the remainder of the day and night has to be prepared to turn out at short notice. Headquarters and 3 Companies billeted in houses and A Company lived in dug outs round RED BARN with 1 Platoon and Machine Gun Section in a 100 ft Culvert, filled with straw. 85 Admittances to hospital, majority of cases for sore feet.	
Nov. 26th, 27th RED BARN Nov 28th A Lines.	Billets. Relieved 2nd Sherwood Foresters in A Lines. 1 Company 5th BLACK WATCH attached to Battalion, and ordered to take over A Company's trenches. A Company occupied partly dug support trench behind D Company. A Company spent whole night improving trench	

Army Form C. 2118.
19

WAR DIARY
or
INTELLIGENCE SUMMARY.
(Erase heading not required.)

Hour, Date, Place	Summary of Events and Information	Remarks and References to Appendices
November 28 (cont). A lines	and in endeavouring to make dug outs, but as trench was in a ditch every dug out filled with water as soon as it was dug. Sufficient cover however for 2 Platoons was constructed during the night.	Casualties Killed Nil Wounded Nil
November 29th A lines	2 Platoons A Company moved back to Batt. Headquarters and billeted near 1st Aid Post, and were employed in improving the communications between Headquarters and the trenches. Trenches getting very muddy in places mud is a foot deep.	29 Casualties Killed 1 Officer 1 OR Wounded 5.
November 30th "A" lines	Germans sent bombs into the right Platoon at B Coy and the left Platoon of D Company. The trench occupied by right Platoon of B Company is known as PORT ARTHUR	Casualties Nil Killed 3 Wounded
December 1st A lines.	Relieved from trenches and marched by Companies to	

1st Bn Worcestershire Regiment

Appendix 1

Roll of Officers who proceeded with above Battalion on Active Service on 5th November 1914

Rank	Name	Appointment or Company	Remarks
Lt. Col	A E Lascelles	Comdg Officer	
Major	E C F Wodehouse DSO	2nd in Command	
Capt & Adjt	J F S Winnington	Adjutant	
Lieut	K W Wilkins	Machine Gun	
"	E L G Lawrence	Transport Officer	
"	C Henson	Qr. Mr.	
"	A J Gilchrist	M.O. i/c	
Captain	F M Tyrwhitt	"A" Company	
"	J Fitzjohn	"	
Lieut	J S Veasey	"	
"	H Fitz M Stacke	"	
"	F C Roberts	"	
Lieut	D King	"	
Major	G C Lambton DSO	"B" Company	
Captain	C S Linton	"	
Lieut	J M Monk	"	
"	L G Phillips	"	
Lieut	H P Hartnoll	"	
"	F Darby	"	
Captain	C Richardson	"C" Company	
"	J H Arden	"	
Lieut	L H Ruck	"	
"	J H Trustram	"	
"	M A Hamilton-Cox	"	
Lieut	F W Young	"	
Major	B H W Bacon	"D" Company	
Captain	J H Pardoe	"	
"	C F G Crawford	"	
Lieut	J F Leman	"	
"	K M Slater	"	
"	E B Conybeare	"	

J S Veasey Lieut & Adjt
1/Worcester R.

Dispositions of Companies 1st Bn Worcestershire Regt on November 14th 1914.

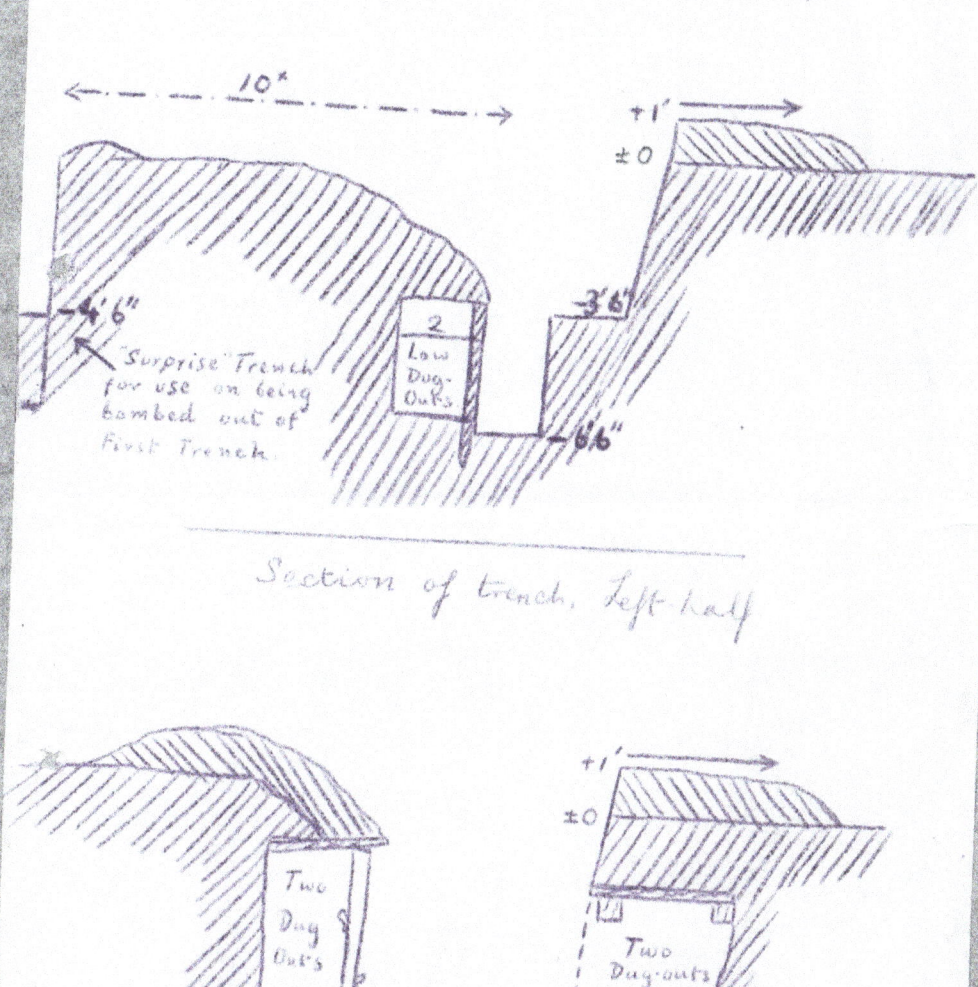

8th Division
24th Inf. Bde

WAR DIARY

1st WORCESTERSHIRE

December

1914

WAR DIARY
or
INTELLIGENCE SUMMARY.
(Erase heading not required.)

Army Form C. 2118
20

Hour, Date, Place	Summary of Events and Information	Remarks and References to Appendices
December 2nd, 3rd, 4th	Divisional Reserve Billets at LA GORGUE Billets at LA GORGUE. Every man in the Battalion was given a Bath in a large laundry in ESTAIRES. [Men bathed ten at a time in large vats, while they bathed their coats & houses were ironed, and they received a clean set of underclothing after the bath] 100 men admitted to hospital mostly with bad feet.	
A Coies December 4th	Relieved 2/ Sherwood Foresters in A Lines. One Company 5th Black Watch attached to Battalion and occupied D Company's trenches. D Company occupying the support trench immediately in rear of the Black Watch.	Strength in Trenches. 20 officers 492 O.R.
Dec. 5th, 6th, 7th A Lines	Remained in trenches; less shelling than previously. We appear to have established a considerable preponderance of Artillery over the Germans, in fact the Germans only appear to be using field guns against us.	Casualties during Period 2 Killed 7 Wounded.
		29

Army Form C. 2118.

21

WAR DIARY
or
INTELLIGENCE SUMMARY.
(Erase heading not required.)

Instructions regarding War Diaries and Intelligence Summaries are contained in F. S. Regs., Part II. and the Staff Manual respectively. Title pages will be prepared in manuscript.

Hour, Date, Place	Summary of Events and Information	Remarks and References to Appendices
December 7th. RED BARN	Relieved from trenches and marched by Companies to Brigade Reserve Billets at RED BARN.	
December 8th.	2nd Reinforcement arrived Captain T.L. Watson 104 other ranks, all these men had been left behind by the Battalion at HURSLEY	2nd Reinforcement 1. Offr 104 O.R.
Dec 8th, 9th, 10th	Remained in Brigade Reserve Billets.	
December 10. A Lines	Took over A lines trenches, 1 Company Black Watch, and 1 Squadron Northamptonshire Yeomanry attached to the Battalion. Battalion was disposed as under. 3 Platoons A Coy / 1 Troop N.Y / C Company / 1 Troop N.Y / 1 Coy B/Watch / 2 Troop N.Y / D Coy 1 Plat A / 2 Plat B Coy / 1 Plat D Two Platoons B Company were killed near Battalion Headquarters	Casualties Killed nil Wounded nil
Dec 11th, 12, 13	On 12 Lieut. H.P. Hartnoll shot in the head and killed.	Casualties Killed 6. Wounded 5.

Army Form C. 2118.

22

WAR DIARY
or
INTELLIGENCE SUMMARY.
(Erase heading not required.)

Instructions regarding War Diaries and Intelligence Summaries are contained in F. S. Regs., Part II. and the Staff Manual respectively. Title pages will be prepared in manuscript.

Hour, Date, Place	Summary of Events and Information	Remarks and References to Appendices
December 13th 1914.	On 13th Major B.K.W. Bacon was shot in the head and killed.	Casualties Killed 2 Officers. 4 O.R 5 wounded.
December 13th	23rd Brigade relieved 24th Brigade in trenches. We were relieved by the 2nd Middlesex Regt, who had great difficulty in relieving owing to the muddy state of the trenches, what snow it about impossible to use them. Battalion marched by Companies to LA GORGUE	29th
December 14th.	24th Brigade became Corps Reserve. Battalion marched at noon to ESTAIRES (2 miles) and billeted (in a linen factory) on the Northern outskirts of ESTAIRES. Battalion ordered to be ready to move at "short notice."	
Dec 14th 15.16.17. 18.	Remained in Billets.	
December 17th	Draft of 300 N.C.Os and men joined Battalion at 3Pm.	3rd Draft 300 R.& F
December 18th 1Pm	Orders received to parade at 2 Pm.	
2 Pm.	Battalion marched to 7.A divies Headquarters arriving at about 4.15 P.M. – Companies remained	

Army Form C. 2118.

23

WAR DIARY
or
INTELLIGENCE SUMMARY.
(*Erase heading not required.*)

Instructions regarding War Diaries and Intelligence Summaries are contained in F. S. Regs., Part II. and the Staff Manual respectively. Title pages will be prepared in manuscript.

Hour, Date, Place	Summary of Events and Information	Remarks and References to Appendices
December 18th	Through the night in close billets in the houses around A Lines Headquarters and was in support to "A" Lines. An attack was made in the evening by the 2nd Devonshire Regiment in D Lines against the German trenches)	
December 19th 7.30 am	Battalion marched back to Billets in ESTAIRES	≈ 9
2.30 P.M	Battalion marched to ROUGE CROIX, and from that point Companies marched independently and relieved the 2nd Scottish Rifles in "B" Lines. Sketch No 2 shews the disposition of Companies in B Lines, Headquarters 1st Aid Post &c. The relief was carried out very slowly owing to the extraordinarily muddy state of the ~~ditches~~ trenches and communication ~~ditches~~ and communication. On this last night Companies not knowing the country used the communication trenches instead	

B Lines

Army Form C. 2118

WAR DIARY
or
INTELLIGENCE SUMMARY.
(Erase heading not required.)

Instructions regarding War Diaries and Intelligence Summaries are contained in F.S. Regs., Part II. and the Staff Manual respectively. Title pages will be prepared in manuscript.

Hour, Date, Place	Summary of Events and Information	Remarks and references to Appendices
B Lines	of moving across the open. The trenches in B lines were much the same as those of the two right sections of A lines, but there were no "dug outs". Consequently men had to remain in the rain all night and day. Battalion Headquarters are shown on Sketch II. By day they were in dug outs owing to shell fire, but by night the farm house was used — it was hardly a healthy billet owing to there being a dead cow in the "parlour". The communications between Headquarters and the trenches were equally bad as those in A lines, only one route being possible by day i.e. across the open from Headquarters to point A shown by chain dotted line on Sketch No 2; from point A a ditch is used for about 200 yards up to RUE DE TILLELOY. Across the road, and then	2.?

Roto?

Army Form C. 2118.

25

WAR DIARY
or
INTELLIGENCE SUMMARY.
(Erase heading not required.)

Hour, Date, Place	Summary of Events and Information	Remarks and references to Appendices
B Lines	via High Street to C Company and thence along the fire trench to either flank.	
	High Street is a deep ditch which was dry at this time and afforded excellent cover throughout its length. It will be seen that for the most part this means of communication is under fire, but actually very few casualties have occurred in making use of it.	29
	The remaining communication trenches, DEAD COW LANE – CHIMNEY CRESCENT – RUTLAND ROW were good trenches but could only be used by night; as to reach them it was necessary to use RUE DE TILLELOY in the case of the first latter and the main ESTAIRES—LA BASSÉE ROAD, both of which are bullet-swept.	
	The 1st Aid Post it will be noticed was a considerable distance from the trenches, the wounded	

Army Form C. 2118

WAR DIARY
or
INTELLIGENCE SUMMARY.
(Erase heading not required.)

Instructions regarding War Diaries and Intelligence Summaries are contained in F.S. Regs., Part II. and the Staff Manual respectively. Title pages will be prepared in manuscript.

Hour, Date, Place	Summary of Events and Information	Remarks and references to Appendices
B lines December 19th.	As on A lines were only taken out of the trenches by night, except in special cases requiring immediate treatment. The medical officer had orders not to go down to the trenches to attend to cases. The German trenches varied from 300 yards to 80 yards in front of our trenches – being closest opposite the two right hand platoons of B Company.	Casualties Dec 19th 2 killed 2 wounded.
B lines December 20th & 21st	Remained in trenches, two Companies occupied in making shelters and improving the trenches generally. It was not found feasible to construct shelters capable of withstanding shrapnel, consequently protection against weather only was attempted. Relieved by 2nd Northamptonshire Regt and marched to billets at LA GORGUE.	Casualties Dec 20th 1 killed 6 wounded Casualties Dec 21st Not killed 9 wounded.
LA GORGUE B lines December 22nd.	When in billets at LA GORGUE, the Battalion is in IVth Corps Reserve.	

Army Form C. 2118

27

WAR DIARY
or
INTELLIGENCE SUMMARY.

(Erase heading not required.)

Instructions regarding War Diaries and Intelligence Summaries are contained in F.S. Regs., Part II. and the Staff Manual respectively. Title pages will be prepared in manuscript.

Hour, Date, Place	Summary of Events and Information	Remarks and references to Appendices
1915		
LA GORGUE Dec.23 24 25	Remained at LA GORGUE in billets.	
B LINES Dec 25th (Christmas Day)	Marched back to B series trenches about 5 P.m. No firing during relief at all. The 2nd Northamptonshire Regt had arranged an unofficial armistice with the Germans till 12 midnight, which we also kept. There was a certain amount of shouting remarks between the Germans and ourselves and the Germans sang English and German songs most of the night which were applauded by our men. In spite of the armistice our sentries were kept as much on the alert as usual	Casualties NIL
B lines December 26th	Practically no firing on either side all day, one Artillery however fired a few rounds during the morning.	Casualties 1 wounded
B lines December 27th	Firing so carried on today as usual, if anything a little less than usual.	Casualties 1 wounded

Army Form C. 2118
28

WAR DIARY
or
INTELLIGENCE SUMMARY.
(Erase heading not required.)

Instructions regarding War Diaries and Intelligence Summaries are contained in F.S. Regs., Part II. and the Staff Manual respectively. Title pages will be prepared in manuscript.

Hour, Date, Place	Summary of Events and Information	Remarks and references to Appendices
B. Lines December 28th	Normal conditions again in the trenches.	Casualties 3 wounded.
6 P.M.	Relieved and billeted at RED BARN	
RED BARN Dec. 29th & 30th	RED BARN	
RED BARN Dec 31st	Lieutenant Colonel A.E. Lascelles went home on three weeks sick leave, suffering from general debility. Major E.C.F Woodhouse D.S.O took over command of the Battalion.	- 9 -
	Major J.S Warmington became Senior Major Lieutenant J.S Neasey took over duties of acting Adjutant.	
6 P.M.	Relieved to B lines trenches.	Casualties 0 wounded.
	Battalion Headquarters now situated at LIME KILN, and as the old dug outs were becoming full of water new dug outs were made in the garden of the LIME KILN. Battalion Headquarters christened "OLDE BARRIER BAR".	
11.15 P.M.	Being the German midnight they opened rapid fire	

Army Form C. 2118.

29

WAR DIARY
or
INTELLIGENCE SUMMARY.
(Erase heading not required.)

Instructions regarding War Diaries and Intelligence Summaries are contained in F.S. Regs., Part II. and the Staff Manual respectively. Title pages will be prepared in manuscript.

Hour, Date, Place	Summary of Events and Information	Remarks and references to Appendices
December 31st 12 h.m	all along the line which we did not reply to. We opened rapid fire on the Germans. Our artillery also fired a "Salvo". We also fired several bombs from our trench mortar commonly and officially known as "ARCHIBALD". It was invented by Capt Peere R.E. and consists of an iron drain pipe about 2 feet long with a butt end. It fires a javelin filled with gun cotton and iron rivets and nails. Black blasting powder is used as the charge, which is ignited by a piece of slow fuse driven a track into the touch hole.	29

Army Form C. 2118

30

WAR DIARY
or
INTELLIGENCE SUMMARY

(Erase heading not required.)

Hour, Date, Place	Summary of Events and Information	Remarks and references to Appendices
	Resumé. Weather conditions up to Dec 31st 1915 with regard to their effect on the state of the trenches. 29 & 30	

From November 14th to about December 20th the weather was decidedly changeable, the wind was chiefly from the south west and occasionally veered to the north. In November the northerly winds were cold but not the southerly. Later on in December the southerly wind became extremely cold apparently caused by their passage over the stage.

The rainfall during this period was not heavy. On an average a rain fell on one day in three consequently the ditches were not at this time full of water.

Communication trenches in the majority of cases were not much in ditches, but the rain and constant traffic made the trenches decidedly sticky and difficult to walk in and it was afterward necessary to improve the bottoms. This was done in a variety of ways namely — fascines, planks and doors were laid in the trenches and in some cases trench mats and tiles were used.

Straw was also used to a great extent for this purpose especially in the "bays" and "dutch" behind. About this, which about the end of December became about 1 foot deep in sticky clay which rendered it almost impassable. Straw mats which are used by farmers for shielding tobacco were first used. These however soon became useless and brushwood and short fascines were then used but these too became useless in

WAR DIARY
or
INTELLIGENCE SUMMARY
(Erase heading not required.)

Army Form C. 2118
31

Hour, Date, Place	Summary of Events and Information	Remarks and references to Appendices

their turn as the clay got over the top and walking become extremely difficult. Finally straw was used and this was sent to us & left deep all the way along about 2 o'clock being mud, then made an excellent footway for about a fortnight and the "long stretch" was still passable when we left "A" lines on 19th December 1914.

The five trenches were still more difficult to keep dry owing to the lack of necessary material in the vicinity to improve them. Planks, doors were used where available, otherwise the usual method was to scrape off the wet clay from the bottom of the trench and to throw it over the rear parapet which soon became 1 feet high and dry earth from the sides of the trench was then put down in the bottom of the trench. This method however had the disadvantage of considerably widening the trench.

In parts particularly in "A" Companies trench there was so much water in the front trench that the above method was unavailing and so the case a ditch was dug in rear of the trench and water was allowed to collect in it and then periodically baled out.

December 20th to 31st 1914.

During this period the battalion was occupying "B" lines and the weather took

Army Form C. 2118
32

WAR DIARY
or
INTELLIGENCE SUMMARY
(Erase heading not required.)

Hour, Date, Place	Summary of Events and Information	Remarks and references to Appendices
	a decided change for the worse, rain falling practically every day which rapidly made the communication trenches, which had been constructed in ditches, impassable with 3 feet of water. Consequently new zig zag communication trenches were dug by the side of the old ones and drained into them.	29
1st August	which had previously been used by Headquarters filled with water and fresh ones had to be dug at a lesser depth.	
	By the end of the year all the ditches in the district became full of water, and it was found that they could not no longer be employed as communication trenches.	

Wodehouse Major
Cmdg 1st Worcester Regt.

"ARCHIBALD."

Cross-section of Base, showing touch-hole and crevice for powder.

Weight of bomb ... 2 lbs 2 oz
Extreme Range .... 250.*

RIGHT SECTION 8ᵀᴴ DIVISION.

Sketch Nº II

SECRET

German trenches traced in from photograph taken from aeroplane.

Labels visible on map: St Vaast, To Estaires, Rouge Croix, Pont Logy, Rue de Tilleloy, The Link, Neuve Chapelle, Rue du Bois, les Brulot, Bois du Biez, Ferme la Barbée

Nº 3 Section, 1st Fd Coy. R.E. (64). Scale 1/10000

XXIII 8th Division 12/7636

24/23

24/23

1/Worcs Regt.

Nov 1915

Vol XII

Nov '15
June '16

12.W
gabret

Army Form C. 2118.

WAR DIARY
or
INTELLIGENCE SUMMARY.
(Erase heading not required.)

Instructions regarding War Diaries and Intelligence Summaries are contained in F.S. Regs., Part II. and the Staff Manual respectively. Title pages will be prepared in manuscript.

Hour, Date, Place	Summary of Events and Information	Remarks and references to Appendices
Nov 1st	In billets in Estaires, attached to 20th Division, as Divisional Reserve. The Battalion was billeted in same premises to the Church in same.	
	1pm. A permanent working party of 235 other ranks was detailed for attachment to 173 Tunnelling Company R.E. engaged in mining operations. This work proved to be very heavy and dirty; with the risk of working out as about (shewn on aerial 33 ff	
Nov 2nd	In billets as above. Working party of 100 under 2/Lt Slummy out ditches &c	
Nov 3rd	As above	
Nov 4th	As above	
Nov 5th	As above	
Nov 6th	As above	

(73989) W4141—463. 400,000. 9/14. H.&J.Ltd. Forms/C. 2118/10.

Army Form C. 2118.

WAR DIARY
or
INTELLIGENCE SUMMARY.
(Erase heading not required.)

Instructions regarding War Diaries and Intelligence Summaries are contained in F.S. Regs., Part II. and the Staff Manual respectively. Title pages will be prepared in manuscript.

Hour, Date, Place	Summary of Events and Information	Remarks and references to Appendices
Nov 7th	As above.	
Nov 8th	As above.	
Nov 9th	As above.	
Nov 10th	As above.	
Nov 11th	As above.	
Nov 12th	As above. Orders received to hand machines to rejoin 2 C.B.	
	Arrived in Nov 16th near ERQUINGHEM.	
Nov 13th	Advance party of 2SS other ranks relieved by a detachment from Guards Division, who had moved up in the vicinity of LA GORGUE and elsewhere.	
	Advance billetting parties and transport moved over to new billets near ERQUINGHEM.	Weather wet and stormy

WAR DIARY
or
INTELLIGENCE SUMMARY.
(Erase heading not required.)

Army Form C. 2118.

Hour, Date, Place	Summary of Events and Information	Remarks and references to Appendices
Nov 14	The battalion moved into our billets near Enguinghem & another Estaires at 2.20 p.m. and moved in their new ground about 4.45 p.m. Billets in this area were newer, and the men were housed in light canvas and little huts instead by R.E. A Company in dugouts close by Madycault, in a farm situated on Bac St Maur — Enguingham road about 3/4 mile west of Enguingham Bridge. We were on a range in the 24th Brigade, but formed part of the 23 Division (New Army). Our dispositions from the 8th Division were greatly regretted by us, and the change to the 23rd Division hailed with no enthusiasm. The 24th Brigade was a Divisional Reserve. A fine cold bracing day.	
Nov 15.	In above billets. Fine all day.	
Nov 16.	Battalion moved from above billets at 4.30 p.m. and moved into trenches South of Bois Grenier. Trenches taken over from the 11th Northumberland Fusiliers. Trenches held I.32 – I.26/1 – I.26/2. A.B.C Companies in front line, D Company in Support (a Pounder) 2/Berkshire Regt being on our right and 2/Northants on our left. The relief was completed by 7 pm. Very quiet. The trenches were not good.	

WAR DIARY
or
INTELLIGENCE SUMMARY.

(Erase heading not required.)

Army Form C. 2118.

Instructions regarding War Diaries and Intelligence Summaries are contained in F.S. Regs., Part II. and the Staff Manual respectively. Title pages will be prepared in manuscript.

Hour, Date, Place	Summary of Events and Information	Remarks and references to Appendices
Nov 16	In front of ch had in several places fallen in. A down cold day	
Nov 17	In above trenches. Very quiet. A good deal of rain fell in the night, flooding the trenches which were low lying, and otherwise damaging works. A good deal of work appears to be put through straight off. Company's Support trenches were in a very bad state.	
Nov 18	Wet and stormy in morning, but cleared up in afternoon. In above trenches. Very quiet. Trenches improving afortnight followed by a clear day.	
Nov 19	In above trenches. Very quiet. A fusillade thrown over B Company in the morning. A frosty night and misty time.	
Nov 20	Relieved in above trenches by 2nd E. Lancashire Regt. A quiet relief. C, B, & B Blts A & B Companies in support from the Jus-t-est of Bois Grenier C, D, and H 2 Co in billets and huts in Rue de lettre 3/4 mile N.N.E of Bois Grenier. Front 5 front.	

Army Form C. 2118.

Instructions regarding War Diaries and Intelligence
Summaries are contained in F.S. Regs., Part II.
and the Staff Manual respectively. Title pages
will be prepared in manuscript.

WAR DIARY
or
INTELLIGENCE SUMMARY.
(Erase heading not required.)

Hour, Date, Place	Summary of Events and Information	Remarks and references to Appendices
Nov 21.	In above billets and Support trenches. Time with front.	
Nov 22.	A & B Companies erected support trenches. A Company moving to Command Post 500 yards West of Bois Grenier & good from behind the post, in which the Company billeted. B Coy to billets at La Toulette Farm in the Rue de la Guernerie. C. D & H.Q. as before.	
Nov 23.	In above posts and billets.	
Nov 24.	Relieved 2/[?] Manx Regiment at trenches 1/3a.1 – 1/3a.2 – 1/3a.3 – 1/3a.4, in front about 1160 yards South of Bois Grenier. O.C. and B Coy. on the line trenches, A Coy in support w. A Coy. was at H.Q. 2nd Coy & from and Stoney Battalion H.Q. at WHITE CITY dug outs, on the Bois Junior – Vir Touquet road. Shad previously been in this day with in front, but they had been a good deal improved since then. On the night was the 11th K.R.R. & 9th Division in one was left of the Manx. The relief was completed by 3 P.M. and was a quiet one. The trenches were	

WAR DIARY
or
INTELLIGENCE SUMMARY.

(Erase heading not required.)

Army Form C. 2118.

Instructions regarding War Diaries and Intelligence Summaries are contained in F.S. Regs., Part II and the Staff Manual respectively. Title pages will be prepared in manuscript.

Hour, Date, Place	Summary of Events and Information	Remarks and references to Appendices
Nov 24	Pretty good when I lay was relieved by 2nd batt. Being trench wet & full of water in winter & large (BRIDOUX SALIENT) dug outs still incomplete on our left, where we were in the left portion of the new front trench commenced by ourselves and 4/Northants in running of Sept 21/25. The ulterfours running were very quiet and did little harm. Fine.	
Nov 25	In above trench. Nothing of moment in trench beyond a little harassing shelling by enemy in front line farrfort and vicinity of Battalion HQ. Fine and cold.	
Nov 26	In above trench. Very quiet. Fine and cold.	
Nov 27	In above trench. Fine & Chilly [foggy]	
Nov 28	Relieved in above trench by 2/R.Fus. Relief complete by 6.30 p.m. To billets in RUE DELETTE. B company in Lemmaned Post (Vide diary Nov 25). Fine	

(73989) W.4141—463. 400,000. 9/14. H.&J.Ltd. Forms/C. 2118/10.

Army Form C. 2118.

WAR DIARY
or
INTELLIGENCE SUMMARY.
(Erase heading not required.)

Instructions regarding War Diaries and Intelligence Summaries are contained in F. S. Regs., Part II. and the Staff Manual respectively. Title pages will be prepared in manuscript.

Hour, Date, Place	Summary of Events and Information	Remarks and references to Appendices
Nov 29	In about billets. Training, with arms.	
Nov 30	In above billets. An exceptionally fine mild day. Command Post shelled about 2 p.m. but no damage done.	

J. J. Gisym Lieut Colonel
Commanding
1st Worcestershire Regt.

Jan - Oct 1915

8th, Division.
24th, Brigade.

1st, Worcesters.

January, 1915.

24/0

S.W.
17thFeb

121/4506

24th Brigade
/8
1st Worcesters.
Vol III 1—31.1.15

Army Form C. 2118

30

WAR DIARY
or
INTELLIGENCE SUMMARY.
(Erase heading not required.)

Instructions regarding War Diaries and Intelligence Summaries are contained in F.S. Regs., Part II. and the Staff Manual respectively. Title pages will be prepared in manuscript.

Hour, Date, Place	Summary of Events and Information	Remarks and references to Appendices
1915		
"B" lines January 1st	A quiet day in the trenches. The Germans shelled Battalion Headquarters for two hours in the morning and afternoon, no damage done, shells for the most part falling short.	Casualties 2 [struck through] 1 Killed. 2 wounded.
"B" lines January 2nd	Battalion Head quarters again shelled by Germans, this has now become a daily practice. A telephone and heavy cable issued to "B" lines by Brigade Signal Section which was put up in the evening between Head quarters and O.C "C" Company	
"B" lines January 3rd	O.C "A" Company reported at 9 a.m that the Germans had dug a sap during the night opposite his left Platoon, near the line of Willows, and from it a parallel about 75 yards from our trenches. [During the night Lieutenant H.F Stocke had gone out on patrol and had put up 3 or 4 Germans who had run back at his approach.]	

Army Form C. 2118
31

WAR DIARY
or
INTELLIGENCE SUMMARY.
(Erase heading not required.)

Hour, Date, Place	Summary of Events and Information	Remarks and references to Appendices
B Annex January 3rd 11 am	The Commanding Officer (Major E.C.F Wodehouse DSO) reported as above to the G O C 24th Infantry Brigade by telephone, and then went to see the Brigadier personally. At this interview it was decided that we should rush the new German parallel and sap this evening with 1 officer and 25 men.	
12 noon	Captain J H Andevs and Lieut Y.C. Roberts were sent for to Battalion Headquarters to have verbal instructions given them. Captain Capel who commands the Company of the 2nd Northamptonshire Regt that relieves A Company was also present at this interview, also Lieut Douglas Jones 33" Battery Observation Officer.	D.J
4.2 P.M	At this interview Major Wodehouse issued written orders to Lieut Roberts who had been chosen to lead the assault. Also to Lieut Douglas Jones R.F.A (Copies of these orders are attached to this diary)	

Army Form C. 2118

WAR DIARY
or
INTELLIGENCE SUMMARY.
(Erase heading not required.)

Instructions regarding War Diaries and Intelligence Summaries are contained in F. S. Regs., Part II. and the Staff Manual respectively. Title pages will be prepared in manuscript.

Hour, Date, Place	Summary of Events and Information	Remarks and references to Appendices
B Lines January 3rd 4 p.m.	The following verbal instructions were issued to Lieut. F. C Roberts 1/ The 2nd Northamptonshire Regiment would relieve our Battalion in "B" lines at the usual hours. 2/ That Lieut Roberts and his party of 25 men would remain in the trenches after the relief. 3/ That the assault should not take place till the last company relieved had passed ROUGE CROIX. 4/ That Lieut Roberts should take his orders from Captain Capel, 2nd North. Regt as to when to commence the assault 5/ That the whole operation was not to take more than 5 minutes and that on no account were any of his men to follow up any German communication or fire trenches.	
4.30 P.m	Capt Capel and Austin and Lieut Roberts returned to the trenches.	

Army Form C. 2118
33

WAR DIARY
or
INTELLIGENCE SUMMARY.
(Erase heading not required.)

Hour, Date, Place	Summary of Events and Information	Remarks and references to Appendices
B lines January 3rd 5.30 p.m.	2nd Battalion Northamptonshire Regt relieved us in the trenches.	
8.15 p.m.	The telephone was established from C Company to D Company.	
	Last Company passed ROUGE CROIX and Capt CAPEL had ordered to carry on.	
9.30 p.m.	Capt Capel reported that all was in order, but that Lieut Roberts was waiting for the moon to be clouded over before commencing.	
8. p.m.	Assault was carried out with complete success. Instructions issued by Lieut Roberts to his N.C.Os and men are attached, but the following is a short description of the assault &c.	
	Lieut Roberts dash his party over the parapet and lay down about 10 yards in front, and on a given signal they rushed forward.	

Army Form C. 2118.

34

WAR DIARY

or

INTELLIGENCE SUMMARY.

(Erase heading not required.)

Instructions regarding War Diaries and Intelligence Summaries are contained in F.S. Regs., Part II. and the Staff Manual respectively. Title pages will be prepared in manuscript.

Hour, Date, Place	Summary of Events and Information	Remarks and references to Appendices

About three sentries were encountered 10 yards in front of the German trench who were entirely surprised and were bayonetted. The German trench was found to be full of Germans who were lying asleep in the bottom of the trench. These were immediately bayonetted & shot and then Lieut Roberts and his party returned as quickly as possible to their own trench, and just as they were getting into the trench heavy rifle fire was opened from the German main trench, and at the same moment the 33rd By R.F.A. opened rapid shrapnel fire on the main German trench.

Our casualties were two men missing (afterwards reported as killed) who had a strain too far off to the left.

The German casualties were officially reported as thirty, but probably were rather more.

Within 18 hours of the assault Lieut Roberts was awarded the Distinguished Service Order and

(9 20 6) W 2794 100,000 8/14 H W V   Forms/C. 2118/11.

Army Form C. 2118

35

WAR DIARY
or
INTELLIGENCE SUMMARY.
(Erase heading not required.)

Instructions regarding War Diaries and Intelligence Summaries are contained in F.S. Regs., Part II. and the Staff Manual respectively. Title pages will be prepared in manuscript.

Hour, Date, Place	Summary of Events and Information	Remarks and references to Appendices
B Lines January 3rd	The Distinguished Conduct Medal was later awarded to No 4725 Sergeant Edwards, No 10893 L/C Darby and No 8912 Pte Evans, the last named was slightly wounded in the head during the afternoon by shrapnel. It is perhaps worthy of remark that although the O.C. 2nd Northamptonshire Regt was commanding "B" Lines at the time of the assault, Major E.C.Y. Woodhouse DSO was entirely responsible for the arrangements.	Casualties January 3rd. Missing 2. Wounded 2.
LA GORGUE January 4, 5, 6.	Corps Reserve Billets.	
B Lines January 7th	Trenches very bad weather, rained hard all night. Found detachment of 1 Platoon at the Breastwork in which has been constructed between "A" & "B" Lines and officially known as "the LINK", this platoon during the day killed a horse about 800 yards behind the firing line. The Platoon was found by "C" Company.	Casualties 5 wounded
B Lines January 8, 9	Two quiet days. Very little shelling by either side.	Casualties 1 Killed 2 wounded

WAR DIARY
or
INTELLIGENCE SUMMARY.
(Erase heading not required.)

Army Form C. 2118

Hour, Date, Place	Summary of Events and Information	Remarks and references to Appendices
RED BARN January 9.10.11 11.12.13	but owing to the weather it was perhaps the most unpleasant spell in the trenches to date.	
B Lines January 11	In Brigade Reserve billets. Draft of 1 Officer (Lieut Schipster) and 145 other ranks joined the Battalion. Lieut Wynter had been attached to the 8th Battalion earlier in the campaign and was wounded. Major ECY Woodhouse DSO went on a weeks leave and Battalion commanded by Major J. F. S. Winnington Ingram in his absence	1
B Lines January 12th	Relieved to trenches, 50 men per Company came out of trenches by day and lived in farm behind the lines	Casualties 1 killed 4 wounded
B Lines January 13th	The old fire trenches by this time were about 3 feet deep in water, and it was found necessary to construct breastworks behind the new parapets, these breastworks	

Army Form C. 2118.

37

WAR DIARY
or
INTELLIGENCE SUMMARY.
(Erase heading not required.)

Hour, Date, Place	Summary of Events and Information	Remarks and references to Appendices
B Ams January 14th	were constructed chiefly of sandbags, and owing to the sodden state of the ground they were only dug 1ft 6" deep. A greater amount of sniping than usual by the gunners, Headquarters and "A" Companies trenches were shelled by a light field gun, but no casualties were inflicted by it.	Casualties 3 killed 3 wounded
B Ams January 15th	Still more sniping than usual. The Casualties during this period in the trenches were considerably over the average, which probably can be accounted for by the occupation of the new trenchworks, which by this time they had not been made entirely bullet proof, and also to the presence of a more enterprising Regiment in front of us.	Casualties 5 killed 6 wounded. Casualties Nil killed 3 wounded
January 16th 17th 18th	In Corps Reserve Billets at LA GORGUE	
B Ams January 18th	Returned to B Ams trenches. [Major W. deHouse	

Army Form C. 2118.
38

WAR DIARY
or
INTELLIGENCE SUMMARY.
(Erase heading not required.)

Instructions regarding War Diaries and Intelligence Summaries are contained in F.S. Regs., Part II. and the Staff Manual respectively. Title pages will be prepared in manuscript.

Hour, Date, Place	Summary of Events and Information	Remarks and references to Appendices
B. Lines January 19th	returned from leave and took over Command of Battalion. Battalion Headquarters at the Lime Kiln became uninhabitable, as water poured into every room. By permission of G.O.C. 2nd Infantry Brigade Headquarters were moved to a farm 400 yards north on the LA BASSEE Road. Rations and stores were still kept in a large farm just opposite to the old Headquarters and was under the charge of the Sergeant Major and two Storemen. Draft of 1 Officer (Lieut C.M. Humphries) and 90 other ranks joined the Battalion and were billeted in the vicinity of Battalion Headquarters, and kept as a reserve.	Casualties Nil. Casualties 2 Killed 3 Wounded
B. Lines January 20th	Rather more sniping than usual otherwise quiet.	Casualties 3 killed 4 wounded
B. Lines January 21st	Relieved in B Lines and billeted at Pont Fixe in Brigade Reserve	" 1 wounded

Army Form C. 2118.

39

WAR DIARY
or
INTELLIGENCE SUMMARY.

(Erase heading not required.)

Instructions regarding War Diaries and Intelligence Summaries are contained in F.S. Regs., Part II. and the Staff Manual respectively. Title pages will be prepared in manuscript.

Hour, Date, Place	Summary of Events and Information	Remarks and references to Appendices
January 21st, 22nd, 23rd	Billets at RED BARN	
January 24th R@ Lines	Returned to B Lines – more sniping than usual. Orders received that no men were to be brought out of the trenches during the day.	Casualties Nil Killed 1 Wounded
January 25.26 B Lines	Trenches – no unusual occurences. Companies engaged in consolidating breastworks, and endeavouring to dry their trenches.	Casualties 5 Killed 5 Wounded
January 27th B Lines 5 A.M	KAISERS BIRTHDAY. Every gun in the Division about 80 in number opened fire at 5 A M on NEUVE CHAPELLE. We also fired a great number of rounds, which the germans replied to. Marched out of trenches to Corps Reserve Billets at LA GORGUE	Casualties 29 3 Killed 1 Wounded
LA GORGUE January 28. 29. 30	Corps Reserve Billets LA GORGUE	
B LINES 31st	Returned to B. Lines, Snowed during the night. During the month of January only 3 men were wounded	Casualties 2 killed 4 wounded

Army Form C. 2118.

WAR DIARY
or
INTELLIGENCE SUMMARY.
(Erase heading not required.)

Instructions regarding War Diaries and Intelligence Summaries are contained in F.S. Regs., Part II. and the Staff Manual respectively. Title pages will be prepared in manuscript.

Hour, Date, Place	Summary of Events and Information	Remarks and references to Appendices
	by stell fire, all other casualties were inflicted by rifle fire.	
	B/Wodehouse Major	
	Comdg 1/Worcestershire Rgt.	

(9.29.6) W 2784 100,000 8/14 H W V Forms/C. 2118/11.

1st Bn Worcestershire Regiment

Roll of Officers of above Battalion serving on the 1st January 1915.

Rank	& Name	How employed or Company	Remarks
Major	E. C. F. Wodehouse DSO	Comdg Battalion	
"	J. F. S. Wennington	Senior Major	
Lieut	J. S. Veasey	Adjutant	
Captain	G. Fitzjohn	Acting Q⁺ M⁺	
Lieut	E. L. G. Lawrence	Transport Officer	
"	M. A. Hamilton-Cox	Machine Gun	
"	A. J. Gilchrist R.A.M.C.	M.O. i/c Battalion	
Captain	J. H. Aiden	Comdg "A" Coy	
Lieut	H. Fitz M. Stacke	A "	
"	F. C. Roberts	A "	
Captain	C. S. Linton	Comdg "B" Coy	
Lieut	J. M. Monk	B Coy	
Captain	C. Richardson	Comdg "C" Coy	
Lieut	L. H. Ruck	C "	
"	J. H. Tristram	C "	
"	F. W. Young	C "	
Captain	T. K. Pardoe	Comdg "D" Coy	
"	L. T. Watson	D Coy	
"	E. B. Conybeare	D Coy	

1/15.

J. S. Veasey Lieut
Acting Adjutant 1st Bn Worcestershire Regt

Order to Lieut. Roberts
by Major C.b.F. Wodehouse DSO.

1. It has been decided to attack the "saphead" in front of your company this evening. You with 25 men from your platoon or volunteers from "A" Coy as you may decide will on receipt of orders from Capt Capel 2/Northants Regt advance over the parapet and encircle the "saphead". There is to be no firing.

2. Having reached the saphead occupied, you will if you find it unoccupied return at once as quickly as possible to your trench.

3. Should you find the "saphead" occupied you will bayonet or capture as many of the enemy as possible; but you will on no account advance further than from 50 to 70 yards down the trench.

4. On a preconcerted signal arranged by you, your men will return with all possible speed to our trench.

5. The whole operation should not take more than 3-5 minutes.

6. On completion of operation you will return with your platoon to your billets at La Gorgue.

7. This Order will be burnt before you commence the attack

3.25 pm.
3.1.15.

(sd) J.S.Veasey Lieut
a/adjt 1/Worc. Regt.

128

Orders to Artillery Observation
Officers by Major E.C.F. Wodehouse DSO
1st Bn Worcestershire Regt

1. You will report to Capt Capel 2nd Bn Northampton Regt in No1 Section "B" lines by 7pm tonight.
2. By 7pm you will have a telephone with you in No1 Section in communication with your battery.
3. Should the enemy open heavy rifle fire on Lieut Roberts party during clearing of trench you will at once concentrate all guns on the main German trench some 250x in rear of their present sap.
4. Should the trench be unoccupied Lieut Roberts will return. You will remain throughout the night in touch with the battery and be under the orders of Capt Capel.

"B" Lines H.Q.
3.1.15
3.5pm.

(sd) J.S.Veasey Lieut
1 Worc: Regt

Instructions given by Lieut. F.C. Roberts
Worc: Regt. to his party.

1. Party to be divided into 4 sections of 5 to 6 men each under an NCO.
2. NCO's + a number of men were shewn the direction by Lt Roberts by means of a large tree behind the German trenches.
3. Party to lie down in front of our parapet and section commanders again to have direction shewn them and were to keep their eyes on Lt Roberts
4. The signal to "advance" to be given by Lt Roberts standing up.
5. No noise or cheering to be made at any time
6. Bayonets fixed, magazine charged, cut off in and safety catch back. No equipment to be carried but one bandolier of ammunition
7. If saphead is empty every man will return forthwith.
8. If Germans found in saphead they are to be killed. Prisoners only to be taken if possible in the time
9. The whole operation to take 2 minutes.
10. No man to advance down the trench more than 30 yards.
11. Two whistles as signal for men to return to their own trenches.

8th, Division.

24th, Brigade.

1st, Worcester Regt.

February, 1915.

H.W.
10 sheets

24th Brigade
1st Worcesters
Vol IV 1 - 28.2.15

121/4506

Army Form C. 2118.

WAR DIARY
or
INTELLIGENCE SUMMARY.
(Erase heading not required.)

Instructions regarding War Diaries and Intelligence Summaries are contained in F. S. Regs., Part II. and the Staff Manual respectively. Title pages will be prepared in manuscript.

Hour, Date, Place	Summary of Events and Information	Remarks and references to Appendices
1915		
B Lines February 1st	Remained in trenches, no unusual occurrences. Our heavy artillery shelled German trenches in the afternoon	Casualties 1 killed 3 wounded
B Lines February 2nd	A very wet day. Very little firing on either side. Germans shelled the vicinity of Headquarters in the afternoon.	
	The Royal Engineers have now completed two redoubts behind our lines, namely:-	
	Post R 2 on RUE DE TILLELOY 300 yards East of PONT LOGY	
	Post R 1 adjoining Battalion Headquarters, which is shortly to be put in a state of defence and manned	Casualties NIL
	Post R1 The works are constructed to hold approximately fifty infantry, 1 Company and two machine guns. They have intense rations and ammunition for three days.	
February 2, 3, 4	Battalion went into Brigade Reserve Billets at RED BARN	

WAR DIARY or INTELLIGENCE SUMMARY

Hour, Date, Place	Summary of Events and Information	Remarks and references to Appendices
B. dines. Feby 5th. 9 P.M.	Relieved 2 North Regt in B. dines. Old Headquarters at PONT LOGY was shelled in the morning and set on fire. It was leaving brightly on relief, yet in spite of this that the Companies all had to pass it, there were no casualties. The Headquarters used by the Battalion during the last spell in the trenches was also shelled this morning, consequently a move was made to two farms away towards ROUGE CROIX. A good deal of firing during the night on both sides.	29th Casualties. 1 Killed 1 Wounded also 1 Killed 1 Wounded as result of Railway accident
February 6th	A quiet day. Headquarters was shelled in the afternoon and a few shots but no damage was done. A German aeroplane fell into a ploughed field which strained but was not injured	Casualties No Casualties
	Companies put up wire entanglements at night.	Casualties 1 Killed 5 Wounded

WAR DIARY
or
INTELLIGENCE SUMMARY.
(Erase heading not required.)

Army Form C. 2118.

Hour, Date, Place	Summary of Events and Information	Remarks and references to Appendices
B Lines February 7th	Quiet day - Germans put about 40 shells into a dummy trench dug near Headquarters. no casualties. A test message today took 6½ minutes between the sentry in the trench and the Officer commanding the Supporting Battery R.F.A. (33rd Battery)	
10 P.M.	Germans fired about 10 High explosive percussion shrapnel shells [illegible] over Battn Headquarters. This is the first time they have fired at night since November 1914.	Casualties 3 wounded
B Lines February 8th	Rained hard about 6 a.m. then turned out about the warmest day we have had.	
8 P.M.	Very little shooting on either side all day. Relieved by 2nd Northamptonshire Regt and shifted to LA GORGUE a II Corps Reserve.	Casualties 1 wounded
LA GORGUE February 9th	Billets	
" " 10th	Billets.	

WAR DIARY
or
INTELLIGENCE SUMMARY.
(Erase heading not required.)

Army Form C. 2118.

Hour, Date, Place	Summary of Events and Information	Remarks and references to Appendices
LA GORGUE FEBRUARY 11th	Billets.	
B. LINES. 8.15 P.M.	Relieved 2nd Northamptonshire Regt. a good night for relief.	Casualties 1 Wounded.
B LINES FEBRUARY 12th.	Snowing in early morning, then rain. Every officer reconnoitred country over which Battalion would pass to support A Lines. Germans shelled "A Company's breastwork in the afternoon and broke down about 10 yards of it, fortunately the particular portion of breastwork was not held. Breastwork was built up again in the night. Very little firing by the Germans either by day or night.	Casualties 4 Killed Nil Wounded
B LINES FEBRUARY 13th	Wind from the South, froze last night, rained hard most of the day. Germans again shelled "A" Coys breastwork which will be constructed again tonight.	Casualties 1 Killed 1 Wounded.
B Lines February 14th	Driving rain most of the day — all quiet.	

Army Form C. 2118.

45

WAR DIARY
or
INTELLIGENCE SUMMARY.
(Erase heading not required.)

Instructions regarding War Diaries and Intelligence Summaries are contained in F.S. Regs., Part II. and the Staff Manual respectively. Title pages will be prepared in manuscript.

Hour, Date, Place	Summary of Events and Information	Remarks and references to Appendices
February 14th	Relieved at 8 P.m., Battalion billeted in Brigade Reserve billets.	Casualties NIL
RED BARN. February 15. 12.30 a.m.	Message from 24th Infantry Brigade received to effect that two divisions had been captured by French 9th Corps. and they say a general attack is to take place on 15th or 16th Inst. Battalion ordered to hold itself in readiness —	29ᵗʰ
RED BARN February 15, 16, 17	Remained in Billet: no unusual occurrence. On morning of 17th ordered to resume normal conditions.	
Bdnes February 17th	Returned to A Lines trenches. first company passing Bdnes Headquarters at 6.15 P.m.	0 killed 2 wounded Casualties
Bdnes February 18th	A quiet day; Sergeant George was killed at 10.30 a.m. within 200 yards of Battalion Headquarters.	2 killed 1 wounded Casualties
Bdnes February 19th	Germans shelled a house used by the Artillery for observation purposes and within about 200 yards of Battalion Headquarters. About 40 High explosive shells followed by shrapnel were dropped within 50 yards of the house. no casualties inflicted	Casualties 0. Killed 0. Wounded

Army Form C. 2118.

WAR DIARY
or
INTELLIGENCE SUMMARY.
(*Erase heading not required.*)

Instructions regarding War Diaries and Intelligence Summaries are contained in F.S. Regs., Part II. and the Staff Manual respectively. Title pages will be prepared in manuscript.

Hour, Date, Place	Summary of Events and Information	Remarks and references to Appendices
B Lines February 20th	A Quiet Day. Relieved at 8 P.m and proceeded to IV Corps Reserve billets at LA GORGUE	Casualties Nil killed 1 wounded
LA GORGUE Feby 21, 22, 23	Billets. Draft of 20 N.C.Os & men joined	
B Lines Feby 23rd	Occupied B Lines trenches, 1 man killed on relief.	
B Lines February 24th	The O.C. "A" Company, Lieut H.F Stacke, reported that the Germans had commenced to repair the Eastern end of the trench rushed by Lieut Roberts on January 3rd. Patrols sent out last night reported that 100 yards of the trench was not held, but that it was full of water, and that there were about ten dead Germans still in the bottom of the trench. Lieut Stacke suggested that he should take his Company out at night and fill in the trench, as should the Germans reoccupy it, it would render the A Company trench in a dangerous position. The Commanding Officer considered this to	29

Forms/C. 2118/11.

Army Form C. 2118.

WAR DIARY
or
INTELLIGENCE SUMMARY.
(Erase heading not required.)

Instructions regarding War Diaries and Intelligence Summaries are contained in F.S. Regs., Part II. and the Staff Manual respectively. Title pages will be prepared in manuscript.

Hour, Date, Place	Summary of Events and Information	Remarks and references to Appendices
B. Lines February 24th	be too large a risk of life for the object to be fulfilled, but instructed their Staff to send out an Officer's patrol with a view to determining whether it would not be better to get in the trench by small parties carrying out readings from our own trenches.	
B. Lines February 24/25th	Lieut. J.R. Cox and 2"Lieuts. G Barrett, J.R.D. Evans and T.F.V. Hotchkins joined from 5 & 6th Battalions.	2.9 a Casualties 1 killed 3 wounded
B. Lines February 25th	A heavy fall of snow during the night, country white until noon when most of the snow had thawed. Orders received that all labour was to be concentrated on again reoccupying the old fire trenches. Companies were directed to commence pumping operations forthwith. During the night about 30 yards of fire trench were pumped dry.	Casualties 1 wounded
B. Lines February 26th	"C" Company were during last night and a thick fog came on	

Forms/C. 2118/11.

Army Form C. 2118.

WAR DIARY
or
INTELLIGENCE SUMMARY.
(Erase heading not required.)

Hour, Date, Place	Summary of Events and Information	Remarks and References to Appendices
♦ dunes February 26th	At dawn, which did not disperse till noon, advantage was taken of the fog by sending parties to work on RUE DE TILLELOY and in bridging ditches behind B Companies trenches.	
2 P.M.	Germans shelled in vicinity of Battalion Headquarters putting three shells into the roof of the old headquarters and two in the house opposite. No casualties.	Casualties Nil.
8 P.M.	Marched out of trenches to Brigade Reserve Billets.	
♦ RED BARN February 26.27.28	Brigade Reserve Billets RED BARN.	Month K.12. W25. fines) 4 + 20

G.F. Westmorland Major
Command 1/Worcestershire Regt.

8th, Division.

24th, Brigade.

1st, Worcester Regt.

March, 1915.

131/4893.

24th Brigade

1st Worcesters

Vol V. 1.3 — 3.4.15.

5.W.
14thinst

WAR DIARY or INTELLIGENCE SUMMARY

Army Form C. 2118

(Erase heading not required.)

Instructions regarding War Diaries and Intelligence Summaries are contained in F. S. Regs., Part II. and the Staff Manual respectively. Title pages will be prepared in manuscript.

Hour, Date, Place	Summary of Events and Information	Remarks and References to Appendices
1915.		
RED BARN March 1st	Brigade Reserve Billets - A north westerly gale, and snow storms during the morning and early afternoon.	
B. Lines. 8 P.m.	Returned to B lines trenches. There has been a considerable change in the distribution of neighbouring units during the last three days. The 2nd Infantry Brigade now holds B, C & D lines. The Seaforth Highlanders and 6th Gordons having moved into A lines. The Divisional mounted troops and the 4th Cameron Highlanders have come up on our left in C lines. The link between A & B lines is now held by a section from each company under Lieut: K W Wilkins.	Casualties killed 1 wounded
B Lines March 2nd	A quiet day. [gunners shelled LA BASSEE Road for ½ hour in afternoon.] Companies working all night in reclaiming old fire trench and in making steps to get out of them.	Casualties 1 wounded
B Lines March 3rd	Commenced to rain at midnight, and continued to rain till midday. Very quiet all day except for artillery fire	

Army Form C. 2118.

WAR DIARY
or
INTELLIGENCE SUMMARY

(Erase heading not required.)

Instructions regarding War Diaries and Intelligence Summaries are contained in F. S. Regs., Part II. and the Staff Manual respectively. Title pages will be prepared in manuscript.

Hour, Date, Place	Summary of Events and Information	Remarks and references to Appendices
B lines March 4th	by new batteries that have come up and are registering the German trenches. A large number of officers of Various Regiments came up during the day and were guided round our lines. A working party 900 strong worked behind our lines during the night making a breastwork along the RUE TILLELOY. 15 men rejoined from hospital	Casualties 1 killed 1 wounded.
12 hn	A fine day. Still a constant stream of Artillery and Infantry officers to visit our lines. We were not relieved till 9 P.M. owing to congestion on roads. Battalion in Brigade Reserve billets at RED BARN	Casualties 1 killed 1 wounded

WAR DIARY or INTELLIGENCE SUMMARY

Army Form C. 2118.

Hour, Date, Place	Summary of Events and Information	Remarks and references to Appendices
March 5th	In Brigade Reserve billets at RED BARN. Ordinary parades as usual.	
March 6th	Relieved 2nd Northamptons in trenches at 9 P.M. Very quiet, great number of working parties & officers of 7th Division visiting trenches.	
March 7th	In trenches. Same as 6th inst.	
March 8th	Relieved in the evening about 7 P.M. by 2nd Northamptons. Same as 7th inst.	
March 9th	All day in RED BARN billets. Orders received for next day's operations – preparations made. 2nd Line Transport parked at LA GORGUE STATION	
March 10th	The Battalion, less Lieut. Compere & 10 other men was in Brigade Reserve with its H.Q. at RED BARN on the main ESTAIRES – LA BASSÉE road. Lieut. Compere was in "B" line trenches & in command of a battery of Archibalds to cover the left flank of the 25th Brigade when it advanced on the trenches in front of "B" line. The day opened with big gun fire from about 4.30 onwards, this bombardment lasted half an hour & was directed on & behind the German trenches in front of NEUVE CHATELLE At the end of this period the guns lifted & three attacks were delivered by our troops, these being carried out by the 25th Brigade through "C" line, the 25th Brigade through "B" line & the Indian Division on the right through "A" line. At 9 A.M. our battalion moved down the LA BASSÉE road in the following order:– B, A, C, D companies to ROUX CROIX a half-of two hour food place, at 11 A.M. the Brigade moved forward to take the place of the 25th Brigade behind "B" line. The battalion was closed up behind the breastworks on RUE TILLELOY as reserve to the Brigade. At 2 P.M. orders were given to reinforce & occupy Point 6 a strongly fortified post behind the German lines which had been seized by the 23rd Brigade.	

Army Form C. 2118.

WAR DIARY
or
INTELLIGENCE SUMMARY
(Erase heading not required.)

Instructions regarding War Diaries and Intelligence Summaries are contained in F.S. Regs., Part II. and the Staff Manual respectively. Title pages will be prepared in manuscript.

Hour, Date, Place	Summary of Events and Information	Remarks and references to Appendices
March 11th	Major Brimmington with "B" & "C" Companies & the Battalion bombers moved off in skirmishing order across the Portail, German trenches to this point. It was occupied by these three Companies about 3 P.M. & immediately put into a state of defence; during this work "C" Company went forward about 60x in front of the spot to act as a covering party. German machine guns were brought up & the Company was forced to retire with heavy loss. At 4.30 P.M. orders were received to return to RUE TILLELOY & rejoin the remainder of the Battalion, POINT 6 being again occupied by the 23rd Brigade. At 5.30 P.M. the 24th Brigade was ordered to advance on the right of the 23rd Brigade. By nightfall the positions were as follows :— 23rd Brigade:—round POINT 6 & to the left, 24th Brigade on the right of POINT 6 & the Indian Division on the right. The 24th Brigade had three Battalions in the front line these being the 2nd Northamptons, 1st Worcesters & the Sherwood Foresters, our Battalion being in the centre, the East Lancashires being in reserve. The whole line was very mixed. About 6.45 A.M. "A" Company, 1st Worcesters, which was in reserve to the Battalion at POINT 18 had orders to occupy support trenches in rear of the Battalion which had dug themselves in at POINT 18 (87)(92). This was done under a heavy shell rifle fire & they remained here all day. The 2nd Battalion Northampton Regiment on our left made two unsuccessful attacks during the day, one at 7 A.M. & the other about 1.30 P.M. To help this	

WAR DIARY or INTELLIGENCE SUMMARY

Army Form C. 2118.

(Erase heading not required.)

Hour, Date, Place	Summary of Events and Information	Remarks and references to Appendices

March 12.

latter attack Major Brunnington who was in Command of our firing line ordered one Platoon each of "C" & "D" Companies under Lieuts. Curlycane & Graham to attack the German line along road (BS)(9C). A position 30× from the line was gained by about half a dozen men; about 3 P.M. the remnants of these two Platoons retired to their original trenches. For the remainder of the day & night we held our original line. 'A' Company being ordered up to prolong our right & join up with the Sherwood Foresters on our right, this Company getting into position at 3 A.M. on the morning of the 12th.

Orders were received about 10 p.m. that the Battalion with the Northamptons & Sherwood Foresters were to attack the line (86)(8S) at 7.30 A.M. on the morning of the 12th.

At 5.30 A.M. a counter attack along the whole line but mainly directed against the right flank took place – the following occurred. The Sherwood Foresters retired right back to their support trenches. 'A' Company of Worcestershire Regiment immediately formed at right angles to their own trenches & brought a withering fire on the German attack, this they replied with heavy losses & charging with fixed bayonets retook the Sherwood Foresters' trenches. By 7 A.M. the position was as follows :- 'A' Company some distance in front of the Sherwood Foresters' trenches much scattered among houses & orchards. The Germans now brought heavy fire to bear on us with machine guns and

WAR DIARY
or
INTELLIGENCE SUMMARY

(Erase heading not required.)

Army Form C. 2118.

Instructions regarding War Diaries and Intelligence Summaries are contained in F. S. Regs., Part II. and the Staff Manual respectively. Title pages will be prepared in manuscript.

Hour, Date, Place	Summary of Events and Information	Remarks and references to Appendices
	at 11 A.M. "A" Company was forced to retire. The Sherwood Foresters had meanwhile reoccupied their trenches but had made no attempt to support us. In the meantime on the left the remainder of the Battalion had repulsed the attack with heavy loss to the enemy & at 7 A.M. advanced under a very heavy fire reaching a line on road (85)(94) which they held for 1½ hours. At 10 am the Battalion, being unsupported either in rear or on either flank retired regained their original trenches, in which they remained until 11 P.M. The retirement took place under a very heavy fire & we lost heavily. About 1 P.M. O.C. Sherwood Foresters ordered "A" Company, (worsted to try & form a position near the German lines. It was only possible for Capt. Arden, who was commanding the Company, to collect about 20 of his own men, with these & about the same number of the Sherwood Foresters he advanced another 150 x & held on to his new position until late in the afternoon. then, as no support arrived & casualties were very heavy he returned to his original trenches. About 9 P.M. orders came that the 2/5 Devons were to occupy our trenches & in conjunction with ourselves & the Sherwood Foresters to make a night attack on the same position. Arrangements for this attack were concluded about 11 P.M. & until 3 A.M. of the 13th we remained lying on the ground awaiting the order to advance. At this hour we received orders that the attack would not take place & that the Battalion was to march back into Brigade Reserve behind "B" lines on RUE TILLELOY. Lt T.E. Fitch took over the duties of Adjutant.	

Army Form C. 2118.

WAR DIARY
or
INTELLIGENCE SUMMARY
(Erase heading not required.)

Instructions regarding War Diaries and Intelligence Summaries are contained in F. S. Regs., Part II. and the Staff Manual respectively. Title pages will be prepared in manuscript.

Hour, Date, Place	Summary of Events and Information	Remarks and references to Appendices
March 13th	At 4.45 A.M. the Battalion arrived at the position allotted for Brigade Reserve on RUE TILLELOY & at 1 P.M. received orders to march into billets near RED BARN where they arrived about 5.30 P.M.	Casualties from 10–13/3/15. Killed OR 3 Wounded Off 1 OR 226 Missing 11 37
March 14th	Remained in billets until 6.30 P.M. when we returned to the firing line & occupied old trench line in & on the right of D" line.	
March 15th	Held above trenches. Subjected to heavy shell fire & sniping.	
March 16th	The same as the 15th inst. In the evening the Battalion was relieved by the 2nd Devons & one company of the West Yorkshires & marched into billets at Estaires. A draft of 28 men arrived.	Killed OR 7 Wounded OR 8
March 17th	In billets at Estaires. One officer joined.	
March 18th	do do Four officers joined.	
March 19th	do do	
March 20th	do do	
March 21st	Strength of 24 Officers & 240. O.R. Left 5 P.M. to bridged billets in Rue Epinette Factory	
March 22nd	March from L. Frans: Rue Epinette Billeted in Rue Epinette on Brigade Reserve. Billets shelled at intervals during the day. Major Grogan took over Command of the Battn.	Wounded Off 1 OR 1

Army Form C. 2118.

WAR DIARY
or
INTELLIGENCE SUMMARY

(Erase heading not required.)

Instructions regarding War Diaries and Intelligence Summaries are contained in F. S. Regs., Part II. and the Staff Manual respectively. Title pages will be prepared in manuscript.

Hour, Date, Place	Summary of Events and Information	Remarks and references to Appendices
March 23rd	Still in Brigade Reserve at Rue Epinette. Shelled during the day. Moved at 8:40 P.M. back to Le Mans. Relief ESTAIRES.	
" 24th	Brigade moved into billets at Rouge Bequin	
" 25th	Brigade moved into billets on the — SAILLY-BAC ST MAUR	
" 26th	24th Bdge C.O.'s arr. the afternoon of fourteen fortunate held by the 3rd Canadian	
	Inf. Bdge. relieving the 14th Canadian Regt. billets	
	The Battn. relieving Section 1 of the line held by the Canadian Division.	
" 27th	Very quiet day. Trenches in very good condition. Communication trenches improved. Draft of 4 officers + 150 OR joined Battalion.	Wounded one
" 28th	Very quiet day. Work of improving trenches carried on.	
" 29th	Very quiet day. Relieved by the 4th Camerons about 8 P.M.	
" 30th	In billets (Armgate) Rue du GUESNES	
" 31st	" "	One officer joined
April 1st	Moved into Divl. billets in RUE ISATAILLE	
" 2nd	In billets at Place d'arms. Good Friday. Draft of 20 joined	Wounded one
" 3rd	Bdg Route march. Easter Sunday.	

Ifsyzen Major
Commdg 1st Monus Knowilly

8 DIV

BM. 296.
   Herewith BN. reports on operations Mar
10-14th as requested.

                          Ruprecht Capt.
                              for Bt. Genl.
27/3/15 }   Cdg 24 Inf Bde.
6 P.M. }

                    Worcester

1/WORCESTERSHIRE

Extract from War Diary 1st Bn Worcestershire Regt., of operations from the 9th – 13th March 1915.

March 9th   All day in RED BARN billets. Orders received for next days operations - preparations made. 2nd line Transport parked at LA-GORGUE station.

March 10th   The Battalion less Lieut. CONYBEARE & sixteen men, was in Brigade reserve with its HQ at RED BARN on the main ESTAIRES – LA BASSEE road. Lieut. CONYBEARE was in B lines trenches, & in command of a battery of Archibalds, to cover the left flank of the 25th Bde when it advanced on the trenches in front of B lines. The day opened with big gun fire from about 450 guns; this bombardment lasted half an hour & was directed on & behind the German trenches in front of NEUVE CHAPELLE, at the end of this period the guns lifted. Three attacks were delivered by our troops, these being carried out by the 23rd Bde through C lines, the 25th Bde through B lines, & the Indian Division on the right through A lines. At 9 AM our battn. moved down the LA-BASSEE road in the following order: B, A, C & D Coy. At ROUGE CROIX a halt of two hours took place. At 11 AM the Brigade moved forward to take the place of the 25th Bde. behind B lines. The battalion was closed up behind the breast works on the RUE TILLELOY as reserve to the Brigade. At 2 PM orders were given to reinforce and occupy PT 6, a strongly fortified fort behind the German lines, which had been seized by the 23rd Bde. Major WINNINGTON with B & C coys together with the battalion bombers, moved off in skirmishing order across the British & German trenches to this point. Pt was occupied by these two companies about 3 P.M. and immediately put into a state of defence, during the work C Coy went forward about 60 yds. in front of the post to act as a covering party. German machine guns were brought up and the Company was forced to retire with heavy losses. At 4.30 P.M. orders were received to return to the RUE TILLELOY & rejoin the remainder of the battn.; PT. 6 being again occupied by the 23rd Bde. At 5.30 P.M. the 24th Bde was ordered to advance on the right of the 23rd Bde. By nightfall the positions were as follows: 23rd Bde round PT 6 & to the left. 24th Bde on the right of PT 6, and the Indian Division on the right. The 24th Bde had three battalions in the front line, these being 2nd Bn Northamptons, 1st Worcestershire & the 2nd Sherwood Foresters. One battalion being in the Centre & the 2nd E Lancers in reserve. The whole line was very mixed.

March 11th. About 6.45 AM "A" Coy 1st Worcesters which was in reserve to the battn. at point 18, had orders to occupy the support trenches in rear of the battn. which had dug themselves in at Pt. 18 -(87)(92) this was done under a heavy shell & rifle fire, and they remained here the whole day. The 2nd Bn Northampton Regt on our left made two unsuccessful attacks during the day, one at 7 A.M. & the other about 1.30 P.M. to help this latter attack Major WINNINGTON who was in command of our firing line, ordered one platoon each of C & D Coys under Lieut CONYBEARE & 2nd Lieut TRISTRAM to attack the German line along the road (85)(94). A position about 30 yds from this line was gained by about half a dozen men. About 3 PM the remnants of these two platoons retired to their original trenches & for the remainder of the day & night. we held our original line. "A" Coy being ordered up to prolong our right & join up with the SHERWOOD Foresters on our right, this Coy getting into position about 3 AM on the morning of the 12th. Orders were received about 10 PM that the battn. with the Northamptons & Sherwood Foresters were to attack the line (86)(85) at 7.30 AM on morning of the 12th.

March 12th. At 5.30 AM a counter attack along the whole line. but mainly against the right flank took place - The following occurred The Sherwood Foresters retired right back to their support trenches "A" Coy 1st Worcestershire Regt immediately formed at right angles to their own trenches & brought a withering fire on the German attack, this they repulsed with heavy losses, & charging with fixed bayonets retook the Sherwood Foresters trenches. by 7 A.M. the position was as follows. "A" Coy some distance in front of the Sherwood's trench & much scattered amongst Houses & orchards. The Germans now brought a heavy fire to bear on us, with machine guns; and at 11 AM. "A" Coy was forced to retire. The Sherwood Foresters meanwhile re occupied their trenches, but made no attempt to support us. In the meantime on the left the remainder of the battn: advanced under attack with heavy loss to the enemy, & at 7 A.M. advanced under a heavy fire, reaching a line on road (85)(94) which they held for one & a half hours. At 10 AM. the battn. being unsupported in rear or on either flank, retired & regained their original trenches in which they remained until 11 PM. The retirement took place under a very heavy fire, & we lost heavily. About 1 PM. OC Sherwood Foresters ordered "A" Coy 1/Worc. Regt

3/

to try & gain a position nearer the German lines. It was only possible for Capt. Alden who was commanding the Coy. to collect about twenty of his own men, with these, & about the same number of the Sherwood Foresters he advanced another hundred & fifty yards, & held on to his new position until late in the afternoon, then as no support arrived, & casualties were very heavy, he returned to his original trench. About 9 P.M. orders came that the 2/Devons were to occupy our trenches, & in conjunction with ourselves & the Sherwood Foresters, to make a night attack on the same position. Arrangements for this attack were concluded about 11 P.M. & until 3 A.M. of the 13th we remained lying on the ground waiting the order to advance, at this hour we received orders that the attack would not take place, & that the battn: was to march back into brigade reserve behind "B" lines on RUE TILLEROY.

March 13th At 4.45 A.M. the battn: arrived at the position allotted for brigade reserve on RUE TILLEROY & at 1 P.M. received orders to march into billets near RED BARN where they arrived about 5.30 P.M.

J. C. Carlton Lieut.
Adjt 1/Worc: Rgt.

8th, Division.

24th, Brigade.

1st, Worcester Regt.

April/May, 1915.

6.W.
12 week

107/5609

9th
5th Division

1st Worcesters

Vol VI   5.4 — 31.5.15

WAR DIARY
or
INTELLIGENCE SUMMARY

(Erase heading not required.)

Army Form C. 2118.

Instructions regarding War Diaries and Intelligence Summaries are contained in F. S. Regs., Part II. and the Staff Manual respectively. Title pages will be prepared in manuscript.

Hour, Date, Place	Summary of Events and Information	Remarks and references to Appendices
April 5.	Earlier, moving in billets – inter platoon football match won by No 7 Platoon B Coy.	
April 6.	Relieved Scottish Rifles in Section 6.	
" 7.	In trenches, very quiet. Lt Cosgrave wood trench howitzer, wet good effect.	One wounded.
" 8.	In trenches. Same as the 7th. Draft of 20 men.	
" 9.	Relieved by 2/Sherwood Foresters. [Took over than trench 2200 FLEURBAIX] C & "D" Coy in support of Sections 5. & 6.	
" 10.	9 Rue Biache (SAO) FLEURBAIX shelled at regular intervals during the day.	
" 11.	In Biache (SAO) 20 dummy done to day.	
" 12.	Relieved 11/Sherwood Foresters in Section 6. In trenches (SAO) Slate of trenches very good & dry.	
" 13.	In Section 6. Lt White killed about 11.30 am making a statement machine gun emplacements a little shelling. Returning to day.	1 Officer killed
" 14.	In section 6. Pte Miller D Cy killed in same place Lt White. D Cy has been moves his down to 2nd line.	1 man killed.
	Go to Juenes Souza	
" 15.	In section 6. Relieved by 11/Sherwood Foresters B Cy in adjourned by tel. Support section 6. ater Cy's OPs. but	

WAR DIARY
or
INTELLIGENCE SUMMARY

(Erase heading not required.)

Army Form C. 2118.

Instructions regarding War Diaries and Intelligence Summaries are contained in F. S. Regs., Part II. and the Staff Manual respectively. Title pages will be prepared in manuscript.

Hour, Date, Place	Summary of Events and Information	Remarks and references to Appendices
16th April	In billets (Btn) at FLEURBAIX	
17th	"	
18th	"	
19th	Divisional Reserve at Rue St. Maur	
20th		
21st	Inspection of the Battn by Sir John French at Rue St. MAUR. The Btn was drawn up in a field to form 3 sides of a square near Rue St. MAUR & the South bank of the river. At 2.30 p.m. Sir John French accompanied by his Staff advanced to the centre of the Square and made the following address to the general Officers and men of the 1st Bn Worcesters Regt, this being the first time possible to say "Officers & men of the 1st Bn. Worcesters Regt, I have seen the Regt. leaving the village of Empenay on the 22nd Aug. for their formation at a very critical period of the Battle of YPRES. Now I think I have full opportunity (services in the Battle of NEUVE CHAPELLE) I must also remember with you the leading men, the John gallant Commander Major Woodhouse & I am very glad however, and so many of the Officers & men to battalion, and the loss of so many others in the Officers' mess have been in the Chronicle of the with distinctions you have gained for the Regiment and I am sure that in the future you will further add to these honours and fame of yours which you have obtained so worthily in the past. Comrades of war I thank the Battalion for such a gallant performance &c.

Army Form C. 2118.

WAR DIARY
or
INTELLIGENCE SUMMARY
(Erase heading not required.)

Instructions regarding War Diaries and Intelligence Summaries are contained in F. S. Regs., Part II. and the Staff Manual respectively. Title pages will be prepared in manuscript.

Hour, Date, Place	Summary of Events and Information	Remarks and references to Appendices
22d April	Commander in Chief's visit and my few words of thanking and individual officer non commissioned officer and man for the past two days at NEUVE CHAPELLE.	
23d	" Reserve at Bac. ST. MAUR	
24th	"	WOUNDED 1 KILLED 1
25	Returned to Trenches relieving 1st 2/W YORKS in Section 3	
	" Trench Section 3 Slight German shelling no damage	
26th	" Section 3. Relieved by 4/W RIDINGS & returned	# xx
	to Div. Reserve at GAILLY	
27th	In Div. Reserve at SAILLY. 'D' Coy in Section 1 met 8th BLACK WATCH	
	Draft of 2 Subaltern and 137 O Ranks joined.	
28th	" " " " " "	
29th	" " " " " "	
30th	Changed Billets to RUE DE BRUGES	
1st May	Billets RUE DE BRUGES D Coy rejoined Battn:	
2d "	" " " " " 1 Pt "B" Coy to Section 2 to reinforce 2/NORTHS	
	Major Auden D.S.O. took over g.c. in Command of the Battn:	

WAR DIARY
or
INTELLIGENCE SUMMARY

(Erase heading not required.)

Army Form C. 2118.

Hour, Date, Place	Summary of Events and Information	Remarks and references to Appendices
3rd May	Billets at RUE DE BRUSLE. Returned to E LANGLE Section 1.	
4th	In Section 1. Relieved about 8.30 P.M. by the 2/DEVONS.	
5th	"	
6th	"	
7th	Billets at SAILLY – Preparations being made for offensive operations.	
8th	"	
9th	Orders for an attack against AUBER RIDGE – marched off from SAILLY at 10.30 P.M.	
	at 1.30 AM the Battn had settled into assembly trenches assigned to it behind Section 1. and on the RUE PETILLON. A Preliminary	
	bombardment of the enemy trenches was to commence at 5 A.M. D & B Coys were in the Breastwork front-line, in D wearing thumbs next them were	
	2 M. Gun Sections and H.Q. A and B, 2/R. Berks. were in rear and next ourselves in H assembly trenches. The 2/R.R. was in	
	support as 2nd line. D & B Coys, close up to attacking Battalions	
	A & C Coys about 300 yds in rear. R/E Covers and (Wirecutters)	
	At 5.40 am the Batn the leading Battalion began to move in breadth	
	of bombardment and R & D Coys began to form up accordingly in rear of them – C Coys began also to close up to the leading	
	Battalion Companies. This latter movement was carried out	
	across the open ground W of the LAYES under rifle and	
	Rifle fire by the enemy in their last trenches, very effectively	
	to this. In consequence then the Coys suffered some casualties	
	in moving up. In coming up A Coy in order to avoid this fire and	
	also because the line of advance had not been previously clearly laid	
	down, took a somewhat more southerly direction was at	
	that instant not the line with the Rest of the Batn.	
	Subalterns that noticed this at once signalled to E LANGLE SLIGHT late on	
	ghost of the battalion	

WAR DIARY
or
INTELLIGENCE SUMMARY.
(Erase heading not required.)

Army Form C. 2118.

Instructions regarding War Diaries and Intelligence Summaries are contained in F.S. Regs., Part II and the Staff Manual respectively. Title pages will be prepared in manuscript.

Hour, Date, Place	Summary of Events and Information	Remarks and references to Appendices
9th May	The attack had up to this time progressed very slowly and almost one appeared to get hung up. The situation differed about remained unaltered till 9 am. At 9 am a fresh bombardment of the German position was ordered took place, lasting from 9am to 9.15 am when our men moved forward to the attack to finish of work Sherwood Foresters who occupied by A. Co. were kept somewhat into part of C.E. and moved up to their's work on the W[?] & to fill up portion of German trenches and the various movements and advances of the Sherwoods & 2/E. Lancs. By 9.20 am this second attack also appeared to come to a Standstill and by 10 minutes time 1st Battalion was getting a good deal movement of in the trenches as men for an orderly deployment and if given in a forward direction too good, and a crowd of wounded was just now leaving communication trenches in rear. The forward position at 9.30 am remained unaltered till 12.30 P.M. with the exception of a steady increase in casualties, a heavy bombardment of this half by both sides, machine and rifle fire continuous, machine guns & rifle fire. About 12.30 P.M. the German guns fire began to increase in intensity with a pronounced enfilading character across our left. At 12.40 P.M. Lt. Col. received the order to account for an intense bombardment at the time by our guns from 1 - 1.30 p.m. after which our officer is to be the fullest chance of this attack as this did not offer to see Battalion which commencing to make being successful the attack which and infantry to attack another the forwarding of an order from Brigade HQ landing a general order to postpone attack to tomorrow the view of the [?] until this attack. The above by the [?]	

Army Form C. 2118.

WAR DIARY
or
INTELLIGENCE SUMMARY.
(Erase heading not required.)

Instructions regarding War Diaries and Intelligence
Summaries are contained in F. S. Regs., Part II.
and the Staff Manual respectively. Title pages
will be prepared in manuscript.

Hour, Date, Place	Summary of Events and Information	Remarks and references to Appendices
Army	[illegible handwritten entries]	

WAR DIARY
or
INTELLIGENCE SUMMARY.
(Erase heading not required.)

Army Form C. 2118.

Hour, Date, Place	Summary of Events and Information	Remarks and references to Appendices
9th Iny.	Soon after 145PM about 2PM D Coy and Bombers rec'd orders to take over trenches to take over from remainder of Sherwoods, who had traces of gutta gutta left in places vacated by the E Lancs. Things had now come to a standstill with continuous gun fire from both sides, and so remained till near midnight to 9th.	
10th Iny.	Soon after midnight the Boys was witnessed not to be replies the trenches up on to early morning moved up into the trenches and took over the supper 500 from Bn Rouse - DE 13 ANC road when it jumps through saps to officers front &c4 about 60 yds. This moment was chosen but reached a hitch and 4 dy by 5th the Bn. occupied Right to left A.D.C.B. to escape observation arose from a successful attack the cause of failure to carry out a successful attack appear to be feeling: 1. On advancing to attack Officers of lygin and deployment from [illegible] and assembly trenches were defective, [illegible] and orderly troops did not face utmost advance of Battn up. For men pushing meant deployer of one another, when with and right angled hands of supposed lines, the retaking great port of a touch. This causing delay in new battalion moving up to advance lochations in file formation. 2. A rapid advance was absolutely essential as eventide tendencies to secure a success, but you a few seasons this advance was impossible. 3. The firebase had not as a non exempt [illegible] with the casualties that was too few in the case of find support rifle to be successful was seen gunn fire.	

WAR DIARY
or
INTELLIGENCE SUMMARY.
(Erase heading not required.)

Army Form C. 2118.

Hour, Date, Place		Summary of Events and Information	Remarks and references to Appendices
May 10th	4.	Looking at the affair lines as a whole the attack was from a salient into a re-entrant, thus given the enemy every chance of bringing an enfilade fire by easy changes of angle on attackers. 5. The element of surprise appeared to be lacking, as the enemy apparently knew that attack was imminent & had made every preparation to meet it.	Total Casualties from 11th to 9th — 11th. Officers killed, wounded, shock 1 — 3 — 1 N.C.O. & men Killed, wounded, Missing 31 185 8
11		The Bn held to above line all day & was subjected to heavy shell fire at intervals. On the night of the 10th about 80 wounded were brought in from different parts of no-man's-land from 7pm to 9pm (11th) & at 10.30 to 1 am: from 7pm to 1 am took places of 2/Middlx, the Bn was relieved by the 2nd Worcest Regt & 2/Middlsx Regt and withdrew from the trenches with no loss. Relief was in ... LAVENTIE when the last Coy arrived about 1 am. D. a/Fy 9.2 men joined concentrated in the immediate attention.	
12.		In billets LAVENTIE & in Support.	
13.		In billets LAVENTIE. All deficiencies made up and battalion ready for action again.	Wounded 1.
14.		In billets LAVENTIE.	
15.		Bn moves into C lines, taking over trenches from 1/6 West Yorks.	Wounded 2.

Army Form C. 2118.

WAR DIARY
or
INTELLIGENCE SUMMARY.
(Erase heading not required.)

Instructions regarding War Diaries and Intelligence Summaries are contained in F.S. Regs., Part II and the Staff Manual respectively. Title pages will be prepared in manuscript.

Hour, Date, Place	Summary of Events and Information	Remarks and references to Appendices
May 16th	Brigadier visits the trenches.	Wounded 4.
17th	In trenches.	" 3.
18th	Brigadier visits advances post in our lines, known as DUCKS BILL.	Killed 1. Wounded 1.
19th	In trenches.	Killed 2. Wounded 1.
20th	Bn: gets into billets between LA FLINQUE Cross roads and S. end of LAVENTIE. Relieved in trenches by 2/Northamptons and 1/5th Black Watch.	" 1. " 2.
21st	In billets.	
22nd	"	
23rd	"	
24th	Bn. moves into Div = billets between LA GORGUE and the LA BASSEE road.	
25th	In billets.	
26th	"	
27th	"	
28th	"	Wounded 1. (with working party).
29th	"	

(73989) W4141—463. 400,000. 9/14. H.&J.Ltd. Forms/C. 2118/10.

WAR DIARY
or
INTELLIGENCE SUMMARY.

(Erase heading not required.)

Army Form C. 2118.

Instructions regarding War Diaries and Intelligence Summaries are contained in F.S. Regs., Part II. and the Staff Manual respectively. Title pages will be prepared in manuscript.

Hour, Date, Place	Summary of Events and Information	Remarks and references to Appendices
May 30th	Draft of 1 Officer and 50 other ranks join. Take over B lines (Right Centre Subsection) at short notice from 4th London Regt. 129th Baluchis and some Connaught Rangers. Reinforced by 5th Black Watch (1 Coy) who take over 2 Redoubts in rear of trenches - 8th Division attached to Indian Corps from 6 a.m. this morning	Wounded 1.
31st	In trenches	Cas. for month (only May 9-10) M.G. W.16

8th, Division.

24th, Brigade.

1st, Worcester Regt.

June, 1915.

2/6

J.W.
5 sheet

18/584

8th Division

1st Worcesters

Vol VIII 1 — 30.6.15

by MCL
8/10/15

Army Form C. 2118.

WAR DIARY
or
INTELLIGENCE SUMMARY.
(Erase heading not required.)

Instructions regarding War Diaries and Intelligence Summaries are contained in F.S. Regs., Part II. and the Staff Manual respectively. Title pages will be prepared in manuscript.

Hour, Date, Place	Summary of Events and Information	Remarks and references to Appendices
1915		
June 1st	Bn in trenches	Wounded 3
" 2 "	"	" 6.
" 3 "	"	
" 4 "	"	Killed 2. Wounded 2.
" 5 "	Relieved by 1/SHERWOOD FORESTERS and went into billets in LE FRANC's factory in ESTAIRES as Divisional Reserve	Wounded 1
" 6 "	In billets	
" 7 "	"	
" 8 "	"	Wounded
" 9 "	"	
" 10 "	"	Wounded 1 (by bomb).
" 11 "	Take over same line of trench from 1/SHERWOOD FRS.	
" 12 "	In trenches	Lieut. 23. Cayleur } Wounded
		2/Lt. T.G. Stokes } Wounded
		2/Lt. Faulkner Lee } and Shock
		men - killed 1 Wounded 3
" 13 "	" - A draft of 1 Officer & 40 other ranks arrive.	Wounded 1
" 14 "	"	Wounded 2
" 15 "	"	Wounded 2

WAR DIARY
or
INTELLIGENCE SUMMARY.
(Erase heading not required.)

Army Form C. 2118.

Instructions regarding War Diaries and Intelligence Summaries are contained in F.S. Regs., Part II. and the Staff Manual respectively. Title pages will be prepared in manuscript.

Hour, Date, Place	Summary of Events and Information	Remarks and references to Appendices
1915		
June 16th	In trenches	
" 17th	Relieved by 1/SHERWOOD FORESTERS and go into Bttn. Reserve billets along LA BASSEE road, from PONT DU HEM northwards	
" 18th	In billets	
" 19th	" "	
" 20th	" "	
" 21st	" "	Wounded 1. (on working party)
" 22nd	" "	
" 23rd	" "	
" 24th	" "	
" 25th	Move to trenches cancelled –	
" 26th	Take over Section I & part of Section II (RUE PETILLON) 2 right Coys relieve 2/W.YORKS & 2 left Coys relieve 8/W.YORKS.	Wounded 2.
" 27th	In trenches – Bn. H.Q. (RUE PETILLON) shelled and knocked down –	Wounded Major Arden 2 men

WAR DIARY
INTELLIGENCE SUMMARY.
(Erase heading not required.)

Army Form C. 2118.

Hour, Date, Place	Summary of Events and Information	Remarks and references to Appendices
1915 June 28	In trenches	Killed 2 Died of wounds 2 Wounded 8
" 29		
" 30	In trenches	

8th, Division.

24th, Brigade.

1st, Worcester Regt.

July, 1915.

24/2

121/6160

8th K worion

1st Worcester
Vol VIII 1 — 31.7.15

S.W.
Sheet

Army Form C. 2118.

WAR DIARY
or
INTELLIGENCE SUMMARY.
(Erase heading not required.)

Instructions regarding War Diaries and Intelligence Summaries are contained in F.S. Regs., Part II. and the Staff Manual respectively. Title pages will be prepared in manuscript.

Hour, Date, Place	Summary of Events and Information	Remarks and references to Appendices
13 July	Bty in billets RUE DU GUESNE	
14 "	" " Watering parties suffered for afternoon	WOUNDED 1
15 "	" " " "	
16 "	" " Premature explosion of a shell one B & D coys billets	KILLED 1 WOUNDED 4
	Sections of 3rd Bty, R.F.A. relieved	
	Horse Garden suffered	
17 "	Bty billets Working parties suffered	
18 "	Relieved 2/E LANCS in section I	
19 "	Section I Everything very quiet	
20 "	" "	
21 "	" "	WOUNDED 1
22 "	" "	
23 "	" "	
24 "	" "	WOUNDED 1
25 "	" " Relieved by 2/E/LANCS	
	DIVISIONAL BILLETS at SAILLY.	

Army Form C. 2118.

WAR DIARY
or
INTELLIGENCE SUMMARY.
(Erase heading not required.)

Instructions regarding War Diaries and Intelligence Summaries are contained in F.S. Regs., Part II. and the Staff Manual respectively. Title pages will be prepared in manuscript.

Hour, Date, Place	Summary of Events and Information	Remarks and references to Appendices
26.	Bgd HdQrs Rue Du Bussere A Field Coy at SAILLY. 3rd Divl. Bulls. at SAILLY. Working parties on Support line	WOUNDED .1.
27.	" " " " "	
28.	" " " " "	WOUNDED .1.
29.	" " " " "	
30.	" " " " "	
31.	Relieved 2/Scottish Rifles and Middlesex Regt in Section 25, SP3 S5, SR.	

Army Form C. 2118.

WAR DIARY
or
INTELLIGENCE SUMMARY.
(Erase heading not required.)

Instructions regarding War Diaries and Intelligence Summaries are contained in F.S. Regs., Part II. and the Staff Manual respectively. Title pages will be prepared in manuscript.

Hour, Date, Place	Summary of Events and Information	Remarks and references to Appendices
July 1st	Handed over Trenches (Section 1) to 2/E Lancs Regt. Bn. went into billets at SAILLY Cross Roads	Casualties nil.
" 2nd	In billets at SAILLY Cross Roads.	
" 3rd	" " Fatigue 200 digging 3rd Defence line	
" 4th	" " Ron 16 men of 7 noncs	
" 5th	" " Fatigue 200 for 2nd Defence line	
" 6th	Relieved the 2/E LANCS in Section I	
" 7th	Section I very quiet. No shelling, only a little sniping.	
" 8th	Section I " " little shelling. A patrol sent out about 10.30 p.m. got lost & was fired on by German all got back with exception of 2/Lt Band who was missing.	Killed one St Saunders accidentally with a bomb. Wounded one. Missing 2/Lt A.C.D. Band
" 9th	Section I very quiet, slight shelling during the morning	Wounded 1.
" 10th	Section I Trenches shelled during morning and evening no damage	Wounded 3.
" 11th	Section I very quiet	
" 12th	Section I Hand grenades shelled to nounce dam. Relieved by E. LANCS at 10 p.m.	

8th, Division.

24th, Brigade.

1st, Worcester Regt.

August, 1915.

121/6564

8th Division

1st Worcesters
Vol IX
From 1 - 31. 8. 15

WAR DIARY
or
INTELLIGENCE SUMMARY.
(Erase heading not required.)

Army Form C. 2118.

1st Bn Worcestershire Regt.

Hour, Date, Place	Summary of Events and Information	Remarks and references to Appendices
1st August	Holding Section II trenches from 2.S Gloucester trench	WOUNDED Capt Crawford 2 28/7/15 (at duty)
2nd "	" " " " " " " " " " " " "	The whole of our tour quiet.
3rd "	" " " " " " " " " " " " "	Platoon of 10 K.R.R. attached to 2d Bn in trenches. 1 man
4th "	" " " " " " " " " " " " "	1 man
5th "	Relieved about 8.30 Pm by 2/E. LANCS returned to Bde (RT) billets HQ R SUESNE. 2 Coys RUE D BOYT. 1 COY CROIX BLANCHE. 1 Coy R.BACHE	
6th "	In above billets, with 10 KAR affiliated for training.	
7th "	In above billets with 10 KRR affiliated for training	
8 "	Relieved the 23rd Inf Bde in Divisional billets round Sailly wounded Regt HQ and billets at Sailly Cross Roads.	1 man
9 "	In above billets. Bn training under Coy Commanders.-Weather dentier	"
10 "	In above billets.	"
11 "	In above billets	"
12 "	In above billets	"
13 "	In above billets	"

Army Form C. 2118.

WAR DIARY
or
INTELLIGENCE SUMMARY.
(Erase heading not required.)

Instructions regarding War Diaries and Intelligence Summaries are contained in F.S. Regs., Part II. and the Staff Manual respectively. Title pages will be prepared in manuscript.

Hour, Date, Place	Summary of Events and Information	Remarks and references to Appendices
14.	Billets round SAILLY cross roads – Divisional Horse Shows N of Bn LYS. Rest war nothing.	Wounded 1 duin. Working Party
15.	Above Billets.	nil
16.	" Relieved 1st 1/4 west Regts in section 5. Relief not over until 1.30 am 17 owing to the Bdg manning at the position to L. Bdg was before the relief.	nil
17.	Held section & trenches – good trenches.	1.
18.	"	2.
19.	" Moved to the right gave up left Coy to the 2/Northamptons and took over new trench from 5 M Black West of 6th Convent wall.	2.
20.	Held section 6.	
21.	Relieved by the 2/E LANCS about 10 p.m. went into Bde Reserve. Moved to FLEURBAIX.	2.
22.	In above billets.	1. During working party
23.	"	
24.	" Certain amount of shelling near A Coy no damage.	
25.	In above billet. Working parts for improvement of communication trenches supplied. Casualty, I wounded.	
26.	In billet as above. At 5 P.m. the battalion marched into trenches sections 4 & 5 just North of LA BOUTILLERIE taking over from the 2/East Lancs.	

(73989) W4141—463. 400,000. 9/14. H.&J.Ltd. Forms/C. 2118/10.

Army Form C. 2118.

WAR DIARY
or
INTELLIGENCE SUMMARY.
(Erase heading not required.)

Instructions regarding War Diaries and Intelligence Summaries are contained in F.S. Regs., Part II and the Staff Manual respectively. Title pages will be prepared in manuscript.

Hour, Date, Place	Summary of Events and Information	Remarks and references to Appendices
Aug 26th	A quiet at day no casualties. Enemy very quiet all through night.	
Aug 27th	In trenches as above. Enemy in front very quiet, except for snipers and M.G. fire, no raids on enemy. Orders received to carry out work of blocking my funnel to 22" trench under R.E. supervision this work started.	
Aug 28th	In trenches as above. Front in as above side normal. Orders received to sufficient work of thickening parapets and wire defenses support trenches in rear of forward to 5" deep, with a few stops in front. Emplacements for Machine guns started by M.G. officer to form an flank fire to these on stabs or communication trenches behind German lines.	
Aug 29	In trenches as above. A quiet day and night. 2nd Lieut Smyth Osbourne O.C "A" Coy killed, shot through head. Weather cool and rainy	
Aug 30	In trenches as above. Work on defenses, support trenches continued. Observation posts in rear of bombard mentstld stand. Second Lieut'd Walker joined for duty. Weather fine, cool and windy	

WAR DIARY
or
INTELLIGENCE SUMMARY.

(Erase heading not required.)

Army Form C. 2118.

Hour, Date, Place	Summary of Events and Information	Remarks and references to Appendices
Aug 31	A trench as above. Trenches visited by Divisional General in morning. All quiet in front, but enemy's snipers active. The enemy blew up a mine beyond our right, but unsuccessfully. The battalion stood to in consequence from 5.15 to 6.15. Intervening made no movement opposite us. We fired burst of rifle fire on hostile trenches at 10 p.m. & stopped enemy working parties in front of their parapet.	

8th, Division.

24th, brigade.

1st, Worcester Regt.

September, 1915.

8th Division

1st Reserves
Vol X
Sept. 15

Army Form C. 2118.

WAR DIARY
or
INTELLIGENCE SUMMARY.
(Erase heading not required.)

Instructions regarding War Diaries and Intelligence Summaries are contained in F.S. Regs., Part II. and the Staff Manual respectively. Title pages will be prepared in manuscript.

Hour, Date, Place	Summary of Events and Information	Remarks and references to Appendices
Sep 1st.	Relieved in trenches, 3,5,4P,4Q,4R,4S, South of BOUTILLERIE by 2/Rifle Brigade; wet in greatpart of afternoon. Relief completed by 10.15 p.m. There was a good deal of wild firing by the Germans who (?) relief was commencing but no casualties. The enemy had fired previously about 5 p.m. shelled ruined buildings in rear of trenches	Casualties for week ending 4/9/15 Lieut W Smyth O'R — own wounded 9/9/15 Other Ranks 5
Sep 2.	In billets. (Companys a niche North of Fleurbaix, 2 Companies on the Rue Bataille South of Bac St Maur. Head quarters "D" Company at Erquinghem and J Bac St Maur. Battalion was held in divisional reserve. Working parties supplied for further trenches. Billets moderate (C)	
Sep. 3.	In billets as above. Working parties as above. Rained all day	
Sep 4	As above. Very Wet, with heavy downpours	

Army Form C. 2118.

WAR DIARY
or
INTELLIGENCE SUMMARY.
(Erase heading not required.)

Instructions regarding War Diaries and Intelligence Summaries are contained in F.S. Regs., Part II. and the Staff Manual respectively. Title pages will be prepared in manuscript.

Hour, Date, Place	Summary of Events and Information	Remarks and references to Appendices
Sep 5	As above a fine day	
Sep 6.	As above Very fine. Preparations commenced for an early move forward. Service of advance recommended by officers	
Sep 7.	As above billets. Equipment handed over, finishing of invalids selected behind front line trenches for the move forward. Very fine warm day.	
Sep 8.	In above billets. Working Parties behind Lines. Training in billets. Fine and Warm.	Buried for week ending 11/9/15 M.O.n 1 Pte 1
Sep 9.	As above	
Sep 10	As above	
Sep 11	As above	
Sep 12	As above	

(73989) W4141—463. 400,000. 9/14. H.&J.Ltd. Forms/C. 2118/10.

Army Form C. 2118.

WAR DIARY
or
INTELLIGENCE SUMMARY.
(Erase heading not required.)

Instructions regarding War Diaries and Intelligence Summaries are contained in F.S. Regs., Part II. and the Staff Manual respectively. Title pages will be prepared in manuscript.

Hour, Date, Place	Summary of Events and Information	Remarks and references to Appendices
Sep 13	As above	
Sep 14	As above. Slight break in weather.	
Sep 15	As above	
Sep 16	As above	
Sep 17	As above. Lieut Pratt injured by fall from a horse. To Field Ambulance.	
Sep 18	Orders received to take over 2 men on Sep 19 from 2/E.Lanc. As above	
Sep 19	Battalion moved into front line trenches between Bonnet Wall near LA BOUTILLERIE to Eastern end of salient near 5 Q, holding about 1200 yards of frontage. BOTTLERS and FORAY forts also taken over. A whole of above taken over from 2/E.Lanc. The battalion marched out of billets in Sailly and neighbourhood about 5.45 p.m.; relief completed by 7.50. A remarkably quiet relief.	
Sep 20	In above trenches, when reviewed, to take over trenches from one night ? Coys. as above to just East of BRIDOUX - BOIS GRENIER Road. Relieved in trenches we were holding by 1/2 Lancs at 7.40 p.m.	

WAR DIARY
or
INTELLIGENCE SUMMARY.
(Erase heading not required.)

Army Form C. 2118.

Hour, Date, Place	Summary of Events and Information	Remarks and references to Appendices

Sept 20. and by 9.30 we had taken over our trench lines, relieving 1 Company of the Rifle Brigade, which became our right, and 2 Companies of the Lincolns which became our centre and left. Battalion then distributed as follows: 3 Companies in front parapet, and 1 Company holding JAY and CITY forts behind front parapet. Battalion Head Quarters at "THE TEMPLE" dug outs, to about 450 yards behind centre of front line parapet. A quiet relief, weather very fine.

Sept 21. First day of bombardment of German trenches, opposite front held by Battalion, to be subsequently assaulted by 25 B. Brigade. A steady fire was kept up by our guns throughout the day in German wire and parapet. The Germans did not bring up many guns in reply, opposite to trenches held by Battalion. Whatever was sent by them was mostly 15 pounder misses up with 4.2 Howitzers, and fell on the support trench, 70 yards behind parapet in general. We had a few casualties. Rifaud and Madame Byron fires were kept up during the night by way in places where the wire had been cut in order to prevent them making repairs

WAR DIARY
or
INTELLIGENCE SUMMARY.
(Erase heading not required.)

Army Form C. 2118.

Hour, Date, Place	Summary of Events and Information	Remarks and references to Appendices
April 22	Bombardment of German trenches continued, being slightly just in intensity. The Germans wire and parapet well knocked about by our guns in places, in others remaining fairly intact. The Machine Gun & Rifle fire of the night 21-22 seem little than effective delight. A German fire in reply of about the same intensity, we had upon a few casualties. Weather bright & fine. Wind blowing from us lightly to N.E. direction. M.gs. opened up fire by night as before.	
April 23	Bombardment of German trenches continued as above, and was again effective, but German front line parapet appeared to want serious dealing with in many places. The German fire in reply was distinctly heavier, and in the afternoon they brought up about 2 batteries of 5.9, which shelled ground about 300 yards in rear of parapet generally speaking. About 3.30 about 30, 5.9, shells fell about our front where we had 2 Platoons, making numerous volumes one of sent. About 1 sounded rifle. At 8.7 p.m an assault was simulated on the German parapet all along the line, when not a single rank showing in trenches & leaving their parapets	

WAR DIARY
or
INTELLIGENCE SUMMARY.

(Erase heading not required.)

Army Form C. 2118.

Instructions regarding War Diaries and Intelligence Summaries are contained in F.S. Regs., Part II and the Staff Manual respectively. Title pages will be prepared in manuscript.

Hour, Date, Place	Summary of Events and Information	Remarks and references to Appendices
Sep 23.	Machine gun & rifle fire as before. At 1 a.m. dose day; about 7 p.m. a tremendous storm broke, and rain fell for some hours.	
Sep 24.	Third day of bombardment of enemy trenches. A damp day. Enemy's reply to our fire about the same as previous day. The Battalion was relieved in trenches between S.E. & N. by R. Berkshires & Rifle Brigade. By 11 p.m. the Battalion had settled down into its place in reserve of Brigade. Trenches by ELBOW FARM and SMITH'S VILLA; 1 and S.E. of FLEURBAIX. The Battalion was then in support Battalion of the 25th Brigade which has 2 battalions, was in support to 25th Brigade. C.S.M. Edwards was killed in this day, & just been to the Battalion who was a Warrant Warrant Officer of proved courage.	
Sep 25	At 4 a.m. the Battalion stood to. From 4.25 a.m. to 4.32 a.m. there was an intense bombardment of the German trenches, followed by a dense smoke cloud sent up from our trenches to conceal movement, and assault of 25th Brigade took place. At 5.30 p.m. the Battalion received further orders, and owing to the German bombardment the Battalion remained throughout the day in its assigned positions A & B Coys at Smith's Villa and C & D Coys at Elbow Farm. Battalion H.Q. at Elbow Farm.	
	At about 6 a.m. the Battalion gave relief platoon 36 to reinforce firing line	

WAR DIARY
or
INTELLIGENCE SUMMARY.
(Erase heading not required.)

Army Form C. 2118.

Hour, Date, Place	Summary of Events and Information	Remarks and references to Appendices
	under 2/Lt Wilson was sent forward to reinforce them close to 2.5 Brigade. It afterwards transpired that on arrival at 2.5.B Brigade H.Q. they were at once sent forward to bomb up the German Saps from their isolated line Trenches. During this operation toward out with parties of the 2.5.B Brigade they were surrounded by vastly superior numbers of Germans who seemed to have ammunition Trench Trenches, and were forced to retire after exhausting all their bombs, leaving Lieut Wilson and 15 other Grenadiers in the German Trenches. In the course of the afternoon the assault which had proceeded successfully, was driven back to our own Trenches by strong German counterattacks. 7.p.m. The Batt^n when arrived orders to move up to the Trenches and take over same from East end of WELLFARM salient to the ditch running down to the bomboardment running at the bottom of the horse shoe bend. and also to construct a new line of Trench from our right, in front of our parapet, across the horse shoe bend, and so far to the entire of the trench dead across it, where the work was continued till the [??] Midland. They also provided a covering party	Casualties to the 7th & 8th Sept 21/Lt [??] Sullivan 12/453 21/Lt [??] 21/Lt G.S. M Clements. Casualties total strictly for week Casualties for week ending 2.5th Sept. Killed & wounded (missing) 1 Officer (missing) 1 W. Officer. Other Ranks 344.

WAR DIARY
or
INTELLIGENCE SUMMARY.
(Erase heading not required.)

Army Form C. 2118.

Hour, Date, Place	Summary of Events and Information	Remarks and references to Appendices
2.5	for the Hun Counter A.G. who were running a wire what ?? moment were the trend to cover the new line of trench.	
4.30 pm	By this time the battalion had taken over the trenches and working parties and covering parties were in position and at work. The Germans fired freely, heavily at times from their parapet and some remaining moved amongst the parties in the open.	Weather clement ?? moment?
8 Jr 21th	The trench was begun the night before we found to be in a servicable condition and was held by 3 Platoons of C Coy who had constructed the trench. These platoons remained in position she all day. Throughout the day, rifle + M.G. demonstrations continued with ?? jun fire were kept up in the German trenches, who throughout the day in turn heavily shelled our trenches, (causing us several casualties. Batt when H.Q. was up in the trenches.	Weather about right in morning, but showers of rain.
7 pm	A covering party was in found for the 1/5 Field by R.E. who were in trench to begin work upon the trench to take the place of the French trench.	

WAR DIARY
or
INTELLIGENCE SUMMARY.
(Erase heading not required.)

Army Form C. 2118.

Hour, Date, Place	Summary of Events and Information	Remarks and references to Appendices
Sep 27.	Intention as above. The known front was shelled in the early morning causing a few casualties.	
2 p.m.	Orders to take over the whole of the WELL FARM salient from the 1/8 Devons by 7 p.m. were received. O.C. proceeded at once left and completed the move at the hour named. On Batt. Serre Hen & Light Mor. Bn. also took place at the same time, and at nightfall the battalion was thus distributed as follows: Holding front line from pt 36 up to 4 platoons. 2 way in rear third of Hersshew head 3 platoons. Well farm salient 1 platoon. In Say fort behind Well farm salient 2 platoons, in bty pit behind Brewery 1 platoon. In WYF FARM 1 platoon.	
28.	In above line. Throughout the night the enemy shelled the tenders with 5.9 and 1 Howitzer Guns; single shells being fired regularly at 5 min at intervals. The shelling was nearly all mostly unpleasant.	Weather wet.

WAR DIARY
or
INTELLIGENCE SUMMARY.
(Erase heading not required.)

Army Form C. 2118.

Hour, Date, Place	Summary of Events and Information	Remarks and references to Appendices
Sept 29	In above trenches. Very quiet with a quiet night. Trenches in a filthy & muddy condition from prolonged rain	Wet with wind from N.W.
Sept 30	In above trenches. Very quiet, relieved by 2/S. Lancs about 7.30 pm. To billets in Elverdinghe	Very windy and cold. Fine

Ffrg~ Lieut Colonel
Commanding 1st Wiltshire Regt

8th, Division.

24th, Brigade.

1st, Worcester Regt.

October, 1915.

8th November

1st November
N/XI
Oct 15

G.D. 11.W.

WAR DIARY
or
INTELLIGENCE SUMMARY.
(Erase heading not required.)

Army Form C. 2118.

Hour, Date, Place	Summary of Events and Information	Remarks and references to Appendices
Oct 1st	In billets at FLEURBAIX. A Company in advanced billets at ELBOW FARM in support of 2/E Lancs.	Weather fine
Oct 2nd	Tablets, moved behind SAILLY, North of River LYS. Headquarters at CUL-DE-SAC from the Brigade being in divisional reserve.	Weather fine
Oct 3rd	In above billets. Working parties of 200 men FLEURBAIX.	Weather dull
Oct 4th	In above billets. Companies drawing off, making good known ??. Went to Hamburg for hours in trenches just North of it, picked on with Battery parties sent to Bois de Nieppe to remove in camp there, and cut piles & bundling for roofing abour standing.	
Oct 5th	In above billets	Weather dull
Oct 6th	As above	
Oct 7th	As above	

Army Form C. 2118.

WAR DIARY
or
INTELLIGENCE SUMMARY.
(Erase heading not required.)

Instructions regarding War Diaries and Intelligence Summaries are contained in F.S. Regs., Part II. and the Staff Manual respectively. Title pages will be prepared in manuscript.

Hour, Date, Place	Summary of Events and Information	Remarks and references to Appendices
Oct 5th	In-dour billets. At 2.30 p.m. the battalion drawn up in square side of square was inspected by Major General Hudson commanding 5th division, and after that marched past in column of route. The General expressed himself as well satisfied with the battalion, and he warmly congratulated them on the fine work done by the Grenadier platoon on Sep 25th when it greatly distinguished itself. He also particularly wished to congratulate the battalion, that on the night of Sep 25th, the battalion returned to the trenches after heavy fire & left them after a severe bombardment & charge, and in the course of that night dug a new advanced line of trench right under the front of the German line, and in the parade expressed his own & that there was a very fine piece of work.	Weather fine but very dull
Oct 4th	In-dour billets. Working part of 150.	Weather dull & fine.

(73989) W4141—463. 400,000. 9/14. H.&J.Ltd. Forms/C. 2118/10.

Army Form C. 2118.

WAR DIARY
or
INTELLIGENCE SUMMARY.
(Erase heading not required.)

Instructions regarding War Diaries and Intelligence Summaries are contained in F. S. Regs., Part II. and the Staff Manual respectively. Title pages will be prepared in manuscript.

Hour, Date, Place	Summary of Events and Information	Remarks and references to Appendices
Oct 10th	Left above trench about 5pm and took over left Bois Grenier on the RUE DU QUESNE from the 2/DEVONS.	
Oct 11th	In above trench working parties supplied of 200 men.	
" 12th	In above trench Cpt. Stiljohn took over Command. Working parties of 200 men.	
" 13th	In above trench working parties supplied – S.O.S. Signal received at 10 pm front sect'n in front of BRIDOUX FORT. No enemy results.	
14th	Returned to 2/E LANCS in trenches N·5·2 N·5·3 and N·5·4 & green quit.	
15th	Held above trenches – little hostile shellin – no damage done.	
16th	Held above trenches – Enemy very quiet.	
17th	Relieved about 7·30 Pm by the 2/DEVONS and took over SAILLY CROSS RD trench.	1 wounded.
18th	Relieved the 8/Y and Lancs Bat'n in ETARRES. Bt. 24th Bty temporarily attached to the 23rd Div. – available and 2/west Yorks also under orders of the 20th Div. in case of attack.	
19	In above trench – 2 officer and 100 allotted to 173 FCy RE for mining working parties of above men for 83rd Coy RE.	
20th 21st	3 officer [...] – working parties of 200 men found for 83rd Coy RE [...] own the Command of the Bn.	

Army Form C. 2118.

WAR DIARY
or
INTELLIGENCE SUMMARY.
(Erase heading not required.)

Instructions regarding War Diaries and Intelligence Summaries are contained in F.S. Regs., Part II. and the Staff Manual respectively. Title pages will be prepared in manuscript.

Hour, Date, Place	Summary of Events and Information	Remarks and references to Appendices
Oct 22.	10 killed in listeners, pretending to transfer information for mutual instruction with 10th W Riding (Service Battalion).	Weather fine
Oct 23.	Ammunition expended. Battalion ordered to go into line from 11th K.A.R. between Fauquissart and the piquet (Sh.22b/4-5-6-7.) The battalion accordingly relieved the 11th K.A.R. at 4pm with 3 companies in front line, and in company in forts Elgin, Eylau and Erith in support. An easy relief in misty weather. Trenches good, with very minimum of gathering into them done.	Weather fine but misty.
Oct 24.	As above	Weather fine
Oct 25.	As above	Weather damp till afternoon.
Oct 26.	As above. The enemy entered very quiet, but shelled heavily very steadily in forefront and behind the line.	Weather fine & sunny
Oct 27.	A quiet day but very heavy shelling, through night 27/10/15	

Army Form C. 2118.

WAR DIARY
or
INTELLIGENCE SUMMARY.
(Erase heading not required.)

Instructions regarding War Diaries and Intelligence Summaries are contained in F.S. Regs., Part II and the Staff Manual respectively. Title pages will be prepared in manuscript.

Hour, Date, Place	Summary of Events and Information	Remarks and references to Appendices
Oct 27	Pain shelling went on down in rate and beyond being trying to the nerves. News was quite futile.	
Oct 28	Shelling died down in early morning, but burst out in afternoon about 2 p.m. About 3.30 p.m. the Battalion was relieved in trenches by 11th K.R.R. and went into 2nd line funk along the Rue Bacquerot with 2 Coys. 1 Coy in billet along Rue Bacquerot in support to Bgde Battalion 10th R.B. in trenches North of Tuquissart and 1 Coy in support to 11th K.R.R. in billet at Lamotte. Battalion H.Q. in Wingerie just in Bacquerot. A quick and bit somewhat hindered by mist, the weather being very wet. Enough Inf'y know of what happened on this day, more than 1000 shells must have been fired in the area occupied by us. Our shelling allowed to be merely done in general principle with no	Weather very wet all day

Army Form C. 2118.

WAR DIARY
or
INTELLIGENCE SUMMARY.
(Erase heading not required.)

Instructions regarding War Diaries and Intelligence Summaries are contained in F.S. Regs., Part II. and the Staff Manual respectively. Title pages will be prepared in manuscript.

Hour, Date, Place	Summary of Events and Information	Remarks and references to Appendices
Oct 28	defend the Hyères. It is doubtful if much further "use would be"	Weather damp & calm.
Oct 29	In above posts and billets, into support Dead End: Hougoumont. Masselot by 'C' Company Wingate's Road Bend; Lonely by D Coy.	
Oct 30	Relieved in above posts and billets by 10th W Riding with exception of 'B' Company who remained in support of trench battalion. Remaining 3 Companies to billets in Estaires.	Weather hazy
Oct 31	In billets in Estaires	Weather damp

Hogan Lt Colonel
Comdg 1st Worcestershire Regt.

D.A.G
Base.

Herewith War Diary
for month of March 1917.

4/4 A B Prattefin   for Lt Colonel
     Cmdg 1st Bn The Worcestershire Regt

1/Worcester Regt.

Vol. XIII

131/7930

WAR DIARY
or
INTELLIGENCE SUMMARY.
(Erase heading not required.)

Army Form C. 2118.

Hour, Date, Place	Summary of Events and Information	Remarks and references to Appendices
Dec 1st	In Billets in Rue Delettre. B. Company in Command Post. Afine mild day.	
Dec 2nd	The Battalion marched out of Billets at 5.30 relieving 2/E. Lancs in 31.1 – 31.2 – 31.3 – 31.4 – 31.5. D Coy in 31.1 and 31.2 – A Coy 31.3 and 31.4 – C Coy 31.4 and 31.5 B Company in Support at Stairway Post – Emma Post – Earlwork at Hudson's Bay, and remainder 1½ platoon in Dug Outs at White City. Battalion HQ at White City. A very quiet relief. Relief complete by 7.30. The lines were in a jumble D and C Coy wet but livable in. A Coy were in the Bridoux Salient which being very low (....) was half flooded and little means of draining same. Very uncomfortable. A dull day with some rain.	Trench Map Appendix A
Dec 3rd	In above trenches. The quiet we experienced of utmost abandonment, the Bridoux salient, and occupying the old dead line in rear of it. This dead line was part of the old line held by us in April 1915 and though about a scene Jerry was still	

Army Form C. 2118.

WAR DIARY
or
INTELLIGENCE SUMMARY.
(Erase heading not required.)

Instructions regarding War Diaries and Intelligence Summaries are contained in F. S. Regs., Part II. and the Staff Manual respectively. Title pages will be prepared in manuscript.

Hour, Date, Place	Summary of Events and Information	Remarks and references to Appendices
Dec 3rd	Repulse of tungled, and being in higher ground from the ridge in front of by Battalions in our position, on our right K.R.R.s (44 Division) on our left 2/ Manchesters.	
Dec 4	In above trenches. Firing quiet, with the exception of a good deal of hostile M. Gun fire between about 11 p.m. About 30 H.E. 4.2 shell were thrown near White City about 3 p.m. evidently searching for our mountain battery situate near Culvert Farm.	
Dec 5.	In above trenches. Further improving and getting free of water by constant pumping. Firing quiet.	
Dec 6th	In above trenches. Relieved by 10th West Ridings. Relief completed by 7 p.m. Battalion in Rue Dormoise to West of Bois Grenier. Trenches bad straggly ones.	

WAR DIARY
or
INTELLIGENCE SUMMARY.
(Erase heading not required.)

Army Form C. 2118.

Instructions regarding War Diaries and Intelligence Summaries are contained in F.S. Regs., Part II. and the Staff Manual respectively. Title pages will be prepared in manuscript.

Hour, Date, Place	Summary of Events and Information	Remarks and references to Appendices
Dec. 7.	In billets. Rue Soissons. 12 n.c. 2nd in 1/5 Pte. Heref. Bn. Seconded to Capt. Morris - Colonel Grogan commands the Bttn during absence of Major on leave.	
Dec. 8.	In same billets. Fine - Bn. Baths at ERQUINGHAM	
Dec. 9.	Same billets. Companies carried out training - this consists of Coy. & Section drill - bombing - party of 1 officer & 90 men supplied for Contact Section — weather wet.	
Dec. 10.	Same billets - Training - Also working parties sufficient of all Companies amounting to 200 men - Lecture on use of Gas & use of Gas & of all officers & NCOs but - weather wet.	
Dec. 11.	Same billets - Training - Working party of 100 men - Concert held at Bn. H.Q. from 7.30 p.m. - 8.45 p.m. - Lecture on Aeroplane photos for officers. Divine Service at 9 am at Bn. H.Q.	
Dec. 12.	Same billets - Training - Working party of 170 men - hot.	
Dec. 13.	Same billets - Training Working party of 170 men - hot.	
Dec. 14.	Moved into the left Brigade Area. Becoming "D" Battn in reserve billets taken over from 12th D.L.I. Bt. H.Q. B.88. H.Q. and 2 Coys at H.Q.D RUE MARLE. Relieving completed at 3 pm. weather fine. and Cold. On Commanded of Major T. Kohn.	
Dec. 15.	In above billets - furnished working party of 50 from C Coy to load motor Lorries. - Cold - billets very good - Lt. Colonel Grogan took over command of a Battn.	

WAR DIARY
or
INTELLIGENCE SUMMARY.
(Erase heading not required.)

Army Form C. 2118.

Hour, Date, Place	Summary of Events and Information	Remarks and references to Appendices
16 Dec	In above billets - weather dull - looking by CRA on the conservation of ammunition with regard to bombs.	
17 "	In above billets.	
18 "	In above billets. The Bn relieved the 2/Lancers in B lettre line - Major Tuke who left the Battn. to take over Command of the 1/7 Br Regt Lancs.	
19 "	In above billets - Trench being good enemy quiet. weather very bright	
20 "	"	dull and cold
21 "		
22 "	weather dull and wet - Relieved by the 2 E.Lancs Regt - took over "C" billets Rue D' MAPLE	
23rd "	In "C" billets "C" Coy at Chapelle D'armentiers as advanced Coy was shelled during the day no damage done however	
25th "	Christmas Day - Companies arranged for more Christmas Dinner. "C" Coy again shelled and our guns were busy during most of the day the Germans for no committee was quiet Carried out to day was dull but Grey Zenrico was held in the Soldiers Club Rue MAPLE - working party of 50 supplied GRE	

Army Form C. 2118.

WAR DIARY
or
INTELLIGENCE SUMMARY.
(Erase heading not required.)

Instructions regarding War Diaries and Intelligence Summaries are contained in F. S. Regs., Part II. and the Staff Manual respectively. Title pages will be prepared in manuscript.

Hour, Date, Place	Summary of Events and Information	Remarks and references to Appendices
26 Dec.	Boxing Day – working party of 50 men supplied to R E – The Bn. relieves the 2nd E Lancs in F.B. lines during the evening. Trenches in rather bad state down and wet.	
27 Dec	Day about trenches – artillery on both sides fairly active. Major D Vaughan joined Bn: – artillery of both sides very active. HS above trenches.	
28 "	Weathered there during the day – Some of the parapet was knocked down by about 50 + steel in wall by Aley was smashed by part of German trench. Installation of our guns shelling [?] of German trenches. Gas brought into trenches during the night. Draft of 114 OR's joined Bn from the Base.	
29 "	In the evening the Bn: was relieved during the evening by the 2nd Batt E Yorks 69th Bde. The 24th Bde being billeted going back into Div reserve. The An Lebon being billeted at HA LOBE AU H1B and B.25.6. Lt Col Gwynn returned from command of the Bde to command the Bn.	
30 "	In above billets. Div training programme made up, working parties.	
31 "	" Continued training.	

8/23

1st Bn Worcester Regt
Jan / Vol XIV

14.W.
Extract

Army Form C. 2118.

WAR DIARY
or
INTELLIGENCE SUMMARY.
(Erase heading not required.)

1th Worcestershire Regt

Hour, Date, Place	Summary of Events and Information	Remarks and references to Appendices
Jan 1st	In billets around HALLE ô BEAU. In Divisional Reserve. Working Parties in front lines	
Jan 2	As above.	
Jan 3	As above.	
Jan 4	As above.	
Jan 5	As above	
Jan 6	As above.	
Jan 7	To Brigade Reserve Billets - Rue Delettre relieving 11th Northumberland Fusiliers. Company in Command Post in Rue d'Armentières just West of Bois Grenier. A company at La Toulette farm on Rue de la Buzenare. B & C Company with their Platoons along Rue Delettre.	
Jan 8.	In above billets. Working Parties.	
Jan 9.	As above.	
Jan 10	As above.	
Jan 11	To front line trenches relieving 2/Lt Lewis. Holding trenches I.31/1 - I.31/2 I.31/3 - I.31/4 and I.31/5. from right to left. B. on right, B in centre, D on left	

Army Form C. 2118.

WAR DIARY
or
INTELLIGENCE SUMMARY.
(Erase heading not required.)

Instructions regarding War Diaries and Intelligence Summaries are contained in F.S. Regs., Part II. and the Staff Manual respectively. Title pages will be prepared in manuscript.

Hour, Date, Place	Summary of Events and Information	Remarks and references to Appendices
Jan 11.	A Company in the 2 platoons (Nos 2 & 4 sections) with B's head Qrs at White City Dug outs. Remainder of A Company holding Stair way, Emma, and Hudson Bay posts. The trenches considering the time give were in fair condition, with the exception of the Bridoux Salient which was shorting full of water. The third line across the Bridoux Salient was being relieved, and was in much better condition than last time we were in the trenches. One 2nd Lieutenants was on our left, and a bn of Royal Irish Rifles 25th Brigade 8B Avenue on our Rt.	
Jan 12.	On above trenches. Somethings but weather particularly normal.	
Jan 13.	As for 12th.	
Jan 14.	As for 13th.	
Jan 15.	Relieved at 12 pm by 1st Lincolns. One man killed instantly, a Lt. from a rifle bullet fired from down Bois Grenier road. One round in enemy machine in the morning swept it straight down from there trenches and have been several wounded in it. Whilst the Bn. Co. were digging a minnenwerfer in trench dug outs.	

Army Form C. 2118.

WAR DIARY
or
INTELLIGENCE SUMMARY.
(Erase heading not required.)

Instructions regarding War Diaries and Intelligence Summaries are contained in F.S. Regs., Part II. and the Staff Manual respectively. Title pages will be prepared in manuscript.

Hour, Date, Place	Summary of Events and Information	Remarks and references to Appendices
Jan 15.	In Trenches in Rue Petillon. A conference at Divisional Post, Bn. To Little Troner, C.O. conference. Hand Quarters in Rue Petillon. Go above billets by 7.30 p.m.	
Jan 16	In above billets. Bathes & cleaning of Laundry.	A calm hazy day, mild.
Jan 17	do above billets. do do	
Jan 18.	Took over trenches I.31.1 - I.31.3. I.31.2 - I.31.2. I.31.4 - I.31.5 from H.E. Lancs. A quiet relief. A by-over night. Div. orders co'n Lieut. B. boy & H.Qs at WHITE CITY Dugs with 1 Platoon at Madden Bay. Post 1 at Stairway. 2 Sections at Emma Post. 2/Middlesex on our Left. 2/Middlesex (E.B.Division) on our right.	
Jan 20.	In above trenches. Normal	A fine day windy.
Jan 21	In above trenches. Sniping lifting.	A dull windy day cold.

Army Form C. 2118.

WAR DIARY
or
INTELLIGENCE SUMMARY.
(Erase heading not required.)

Instructions regarding War Diaries and Intelligence Summaries are contained in F.S. Regs., Part II. and the Staff Manual respectively. Title pages will be prepared in manuscript.

Hour, Date, Place	Summary of Events and Information	Remarks and references to Appendices
Jan 22	In above trenches. Very quiet.	A slump. Fell day.
Jan 23	In above Trenches. Quiet day. Enemy very trench hd a brisk burst the night 22/23 inst. for they were very quiet until 10 p.m. after that we had very heavy firing. Hostile Arty were very busy around our lines but also very busy Bois Grenier Ave Stella Wulvest E. Shelled about 1 p.m. about 10 shells.	Fine & bright about 4 hr a shortly dark shower fog came down.
Jan 24	Relieved about 7.30 by 9th Yorkshire Regt. & proceeded to billets at FORT ROMPU. Nos 3&6 H.Q. C.O.Y. (Durnurd reserve) Batts in huts.	Fine
Jan 25	In billets as above.	Fine
Jan 26	In billets as above. Paraded as for tomorrow & Durnurd billets with the batts for the night.	Fine Fine
Jan 27	In billets as above. 1st Coy & 15th & 16th Royal Scots billets.	Cloudy
Jan 28	In billets as above. 16th Royal Scots leave for trenches Batts.	Fair
Jan 29	In billets as above. Colts Deur Qune & Wrahanhlers Coys	Dull
Jan 30	In billets as above. 8th Durnurd handstrap in afternoon	Foggy
Jan 31	In billets as above. Rgs Recon billets. Beaus billets for Rgs Recon billets came by BGL Wilshe ore hers U M F. RUEMARLE, FONTERPA billets taken & placed. H.6.D. D.Coy HAC. BRS. IN COL GRESTED LINE HIPPR DE FRIEZ C.COY in CHAPELLE ARMENTIERES	Dull

Army Form C. 2118.

WAR DIARY
or
INTELLIGENCE SUMMARY.   1st Worcestershire Regt.
(Erase heading not required.)

Instructions regarding War Diaries and Intelligence Summaries are contained in F. S. Regs., Part II. and the Staff Manual respectively. Title pages will be prepared in manuscript.

Hour, Date, Place	Summary of Events and Information	Remarks and references to Appendices
Feb 1st	In billets Rue Marle (Armentières)	
2nd	In billets as above	
3rd	In billets as above	
4th	To trenches, relieving 2/E. Lancs in I 21.2 – I 21.3 – I 21.4 – I 15.1 – I 15.2. I 16.1 (B. Coy right – D centre. A left) 6 Company in Bois Grisier line in support. A Coy relief 2/Northumb in our right and a battalion of 21st Div (2nd Army on our left) near Chapelle d'Armentières.	
5th	In above trenches. Very quiet	
6th	As above	
7th	As above. Very quiet. Patrolling sent out on our rank.	Fine and sunny
8th	Relieved by 2/E. Lancs about 7 p.m. To Brigade Reserve billets in Rue Marle.	Showery
9th	In billets in Rue Marle. One Company of 2nd Bn. West Northumberland Fusiliers (Armstrong) attached for instructional purposes. The company was split up and attached in even numbers per Coy.	A fine mild day.

15. W.
17 acres

(73989) W4141—463. 400,000. 9/14. H.&J.Ltd. Forms/C. 2118/10.

WAR DIARY
or
INTELLIGENCE SUMMARY.
(Erase heading not required.)

Army Form C. 2118.

Instructions regarding War Diaries and Intelligence Summaries are contained in F. S. Regs., Part II. and the Staff Manual respectively. Title pages will be prepared in manuscript.

Hour, Date, Place	Summary of Events and Information	Remarks and references to Appendices
Feb 10th	In billets Rue Masele. A few 5.9 shells dropped in vicinity of billets. No damage	
11th	To Tranchées I.21.3. I.21.2. I.21.4. I.15.1. I.15.2. I.16.1. B company on right front German House Salient, C company in Centre A. Coy on Bayor Left. Relief complete by 8 p.m. Regiment relieved 2/ F hano. On our right the 2/Northants, on our left at L. De Rond a battalion of 21st Division. D. Company in support in Bois Grenier line.	
12.	In dans tranchées. Enemy was fairly active all along the front, and kept up a steady shell fire all day on front line and communication trenches. During the course of the afternoon I.21.2 was subjected to a severe bombardment from gun fire and minen-	

8/23

Vol 15

W A R   D I A R Y.

of

1st WORCESTERSHIRE REGIMENT.

Hour, Date, Place.	Summary of Events and Information.	Remarks and references to Appendices.
February 1st	In billets Rue Marle (Armentieres)	
2nd	In billets as above.	
3rd	In billets as above.	
4th	To trenches, relieving 2/E.Lancs in I 21.2 - I 21.3 - I 21.4 - I 15.1 - I 15.2 - I 16.1. (B.Coy. right - D.centre - A.left) C Company in Bois Grenier line near Chapelle d'Armentieres in support. A quiet relief. 2/Northants on our right and a battalion of 21st Div. (2nd Army on our left).	
5th	In above trenches. Very quiet.	
6th	As above.	
7th	As above. Very quiet. Patrolling and routine work.	Fine and sunny.
8th	Relieved by 2/E.Lancs about 7p.m. to Brigade Reserve billets in Rue Marle.	Showery.
9th	In billets in Rue Marle. One Company of 24th Bn. Northumberland Fusiliers (New Army) attached for instructional purposes. This company was split up and integrated in our own companies pro tem.	A fine mild day.

Hour, Date, Place.	Summary of Events and Information.	Remarks and references to Appendices.
February 10th	In billets, Rue Marle. A few 5.9 shells dropped in vicinity of billets. No damage.	
11th	To Trenches I.21.3. I.21.2. I.21.4. I.15.1. I.15.2. I.16.1. B. company on right opposite German House Salient, C. Company in Centre, A. Coy. on left. Relief complete by 8 p.m. Regiment relieved 2/E.Lancs. On our right the 2/Northants, on our left at Lille Road a battalion of 21st Division. D Company in support in Bois Grenier Line.	
12th	In above Trenches. Enemy were pretty active all along the front, and kept up a steady shell fire all day on front line and Communication Trenches. During the course of the afternoon I.21.2 was subjected to a severe bombardment from gun fire and aerial torpedoes. The latter of very large	

Hour, Date, Place.	Summary of Events and Information.	Remarks and references to Appendices.
February 12th	size, exploding with deafening noise, and making caverns at least 15 to 18 feet in Diameter. In consequence of this it became necessary to clear I. 21.2 of men. Our howitzers retaliated in the course of the afternoon but did not completely silence the enemy. I. 15.2 was also somewhat heavily shelled in the course of the afternoon.	
February 13th	The enemy were even more noisy to-day than yesterday, I. 21.2 being heavily pounded with shells and aerial torpedoes. Our artillery replied, and our 6" howitzers came into action, bombarding German House Salient with good effect. I. 21.2 was so knocked about that a platoon was brought up	

Hour, Date, Place.	Summary of Events and Information.	Remarks and references to Appendices.
February 13th	at night from Bois Grenier line, to reinforce I.21.2 salient in case the enemy tried to raid it. A Coy. 15.2 was also heavily shelled during the course of the afternoon. About 6.30 p.m. the company of the 24th Northumberland Fusiliers which came into trenches with us under instruction withdrew to billets. Trench H.Q. was shelled about 12.30 a.m. and a Dug-Out knocked in. A quiet night in trenches contrary to expectation.	
February 14th	A quiet day in trenches, and advantage was taken of this to repair damaged parapets. At about 8.30 p.m. we were relieved by 25th Northumberland Fusiliers (34th Division) New Army,	

Hour, Date, Place.	Summary of Events and Information.	Remarks and references to Appendices.
February 14th	the relief passing off very smoothly. The battalion going in billets near Jesus Farm, about 1½ miles from Erquinghem on North side of River Lys. All ranks were very glad to get out of trenches as the shelling on 12th and 13th had been pretty severe.	
15th	In above billets.	Very Windy.
16th	In above billets.	High Winds. Fine.
17th	In above billets. Working parties to Brisbrenier Line. Draining billets.	Fine and Cold.
18th	In above billets. Preparing for move to Corps Reserve.	Damp and Unsettled.

Hour, Date, Place.	Summary of Events and Information.	Remarks and references to Appendices.
February 21st	arrived in new billets and were thus distributed B & D companies in cheese factory at Moulin Fontaine. A.company in several farms East of factory. C company in farms North of Factory. Hd. Quarters about 200 yards west of La belle Hotesse cross roads. The billets on the whole were fair. Heavy baggage picked up here. A very heavy bombardment was heard all day from direction of La Bassee.	March discipline on the whole was satisfactory, considering the long time battalion had been in trenches.
22nd	In above billets. Cleaning up.	Cold and snowed all day.
23rd	In above billets. Orders received to proceed on 24th to Esterres about 9.30 a.m. subsequently cancelled at 3.30 p.m.	Cold and still snowing.

Hour, Date, Place.	Summary of Events and Information.	Remarks and references to Appendices.
February 19th	In above billets: draining ground round huts. Working parties.	Damp and Cold.
20th	The battalion left above billets for Vieux Birquin en route for Corps Reserve. Heavy baggage had left the day previously in 3 motor lorries for Corps reserve area. Leading Company left Halle o beau Crossroads at 12 midnight Remaining companies following at 10 minutes interval Order of march A.B.C.D. Hd. Qrs. Route taken Steenwerck - Vieux Birquin. Length of march about 10 miles. Battalion arrived in billets about 4 p.m. A few German aeroplanes flew very low over battalion about 12.50 p.m. between Halle o Beau and Steenwerck.	A fine mild day. Ideal for marching.
21st	At 8.20 a.m. the battalion broke up their billets near La Couronne about 1 mile South of Vieux Birquin Church and marched in brigade for Corps Reserve Area near Sereus.Order of march 1/Sherwoods, 2/E.Lancs. 1/Worcs. 2/Northants. Route Vieux Birquin, La Motte, Morbecque, Steenbecque, La belle Hozesse. About 1 p.m. battalion	A fine mild day.

Hour, Date, Place.	Summary of Events and Information.	Remarks and references to Appendices.
February 24th	In above billets. Training.	Cold with N.E. wind.
25th	In above billets. Training.	N.E. winds. Snow.
26th	In above billets. Route March.	Fine.
27th	In above billets. Church Parade.	Cold.
28th	In above billets. Orders received to move to Bruay on 27th.	
29th	At 9.20 a.m. battalion marched from billets, entraining at Thiennes at 11.30 a.m. Proceeded by train to Calonne-Ricourt where the detrained at 1 p.m. Thence by march route 5 miles to Bruay where they got into billets at about 5 p.m. Considerable delay was experienced after arrival in Bruay before battalion was billeted, as the move being an urgent one, little preliminary arrangements were made. No British troops had been previously billeted in Bruay as we relieved the French there. The billets were pretty good, and the attitude of inhabitants very friendly. Baggage and transport by route march, arriving in billets about 9 p.m.	

(Sd) J. Fitz.
C. Gayer   Lt. Colonel,
Comdg. Worcestershire Regiment.

Army Form C. 2118.

WAR DIARY
or
INTELLIGENCE SUMMARY.
(Erase heading not required.)

Instructions regarding War Diaries and Intelligence Summaries are contained in F.S. Regs., Part II. and the Staff Manual respectively. Title pages will be prepared in manuscript.

Hour, Date, Place	Summary of Events and Information	Remarks and references to Appendices
March 1st	In billets in BRUAY	Fine
2nd	In billets BRUAY	
2½pm	Relieve 3rd portion of 2nd Brigade by IV Corps Reconnaissance 3 to 4.5.	Fine
3rd	In above billets. Army buggy wained from NIN FONTAINE	
4th	In above billets	Bad r. billets.
5th	In above billets	Rd
6th	In above billets	Billets. Snowing
7th	In above billets: At 1pm ordered in brigade to GOUY-SERVINS the 23rd division having moved off to take over trenches from French opposite SOUCHEZ. The 22th Brigade moved off first did suffered to relieve Brigade (6483). The 1st Worcester broke up billets in GOUY-SERVINS. Arrived about 3 p.m. after	Cold, Snow Snow. Cold r Snow

WAR DIARY
or
INTELLIGENCE SUMMARY.
(Erase heading not required.)

Army Form C. 2118.

Hour, Date, Place	Summary of Events and Information	Remarks and references to Appendices
7th	A tiresome march via BRUAY — HOUDAIN — REBREUVE — OBLAIN — FRESNICOURT — GRANDSERVIN — PETITSERVIN. Billets found good, but left very dirty and unsanitary; but this was anticipated. The bulk of the battalion billeted in the Château de GOUY-SERVINS, an old uninhabited château once belonging to the Counts of BETHUNE but abandoned in 1793 and allowed to fall into disrepair since then. The numerous large windows (having been bricked up by subsequent owners to save window tax. A good many of these date in after our first visit) but the château itself is none the worse for a stray shell.	Addl.Sources: Tim & Savy Addenda: Appx. B.I.I. Vic.
8th	In above billets	
9th	In above billets	
10th	Reconnaissance SOUCHEZ and BOIS DES ECOLOIRS (map reference 16 A) relieving 11th West Yorks. 3 Coy's in front line B.C.D from my Bn. left A Coy in support near Bn. HQ. The trenches were poor and

WAR DIARY
or
INTELLIGENCE SUMMARY.
(Erase heading not required.)

Army Form C. 2118.

Hour, Date, Place	Summary of Events and Information	Remarks and references to Appendices
	very little work had been put into them by the French who constructed them. They were not much better than scrapes in the ground, of the old 3 x 3 shelter trench type. B. H.Q. in dugout about 250 yards in rear of the centre of the line on the reverse slope of the ridge, the trenches being on the forward side. L.H. of redr. with Germans on opposite side about 100 to 150 yards away. The Battn. was relieved out of billets about 5.15 p.m. and proceeded by VILLERS au BOIS [CARENCY] and BOYAU 130ecm. and BOYAU COBURG. The ditch was a long one as the above BOYAU were well over a mile in length and had to be used by 2 battalions coming in & 2 going out. On our left the 2/5 F. home in our right the 1/5 Dev'n relieved. 3rd Army the last trenches held by the battalion rested on the arras Armentières LILLE road, the extreme left of the 1st Army and the front trenches we were on holding, were the advance right of the 1st Army, a suivre transformation	

Army Form C. 2118.

WAR DIARY
or
INTELLIGENCE SUMMARY.
(Erase heading not required.)

Instructions regarding War Diaries and Intelligence Summaries are contained in F. S. Regs., Part II. and the Staff Manual respectively. Title pages will be prepared in manuscript.

Hour, Date, Place	Summary of Events and Information	Remarks and references to Appendices
11h	In above trenches, a good deal of intense shell shelling, but little rifle fire. The whole country round which included ABLAIN ST NAZAIRE — DAME DE LORETTE and SOUCHEZ has been made in every direction undergoing the fiercest fighting of 1915 in this region between the French and Germans. There will see no absolute second work in visible midst mass of trenches, and took most of it demolished in every spirm spent by shell holes.	Wild & Tramp.
12h	In above trenches. Some shelling.	
13h	In above trenches	
14h	In above trenches	
15h	Relieved in trenches by 2/8 London R.F. A normal	
15h	Relieved in trenches 2/8 London R.f.A normal	
	rel.of Relief complete by 11.45.	
16h	In GOUY SERVINS, in afternoon by march to BEUVRY	

WAR DIARY
or
INTELLIGENCE SUMMARY.
(Erase heading not required.)

Army Form C. 2118.

Hour, Date, Place	Summary of Events and Information	Remarks and references to Appendices
17th	In above billets	
18th	In above billets. The G.O.C. is Chief pushed the Bn. hard during the afternoon. This was no parade - Bn. bathed at BRUAY.	
19th	In above billets.	
20th	In above billets - Leave started again - the Bn. marched to COUPIGNY during the afternoon	
21st	The Bn. took over trenches during the night 21/22 from Bn. 1/Royal Berks Regt in the Bowden I area.	
22nd	In above trenches	
23rd	" - weather very cold - Trenches had to being improved & go up taken during daylight. Slight shelling.	1 wounded / 1 wounded
24th	In above trenches - Bad shelling at intervals during the day	
25th	In above trenches returned by the 2 E Lancs Regt during the night - Billets in BOIS DES NOULETTES huts	1 killed 1 wounded
26th	Billets in BOIS DES NOULETTES - good billets - weather hot and cold.	
27th	Billets BOIS DES NOULETTES - Lieut. Col. Hopkins feeling ill. Col Goggins took on command of the Bn.	
28th	2nd Lt. Roles temporary - Major Vaughan Command of the Bn.	

Army Form C. 2118.

WAR DIARY
or
INTELLIGENCE SUMMARY.
(*Erase heading not required.*)

Hour, Date, Place	Summary of Events and Information	Remarks and references to Appendices
29th	In billets Bois des Noulettes. Relieved 2.E Lancs in Souchez I section on night 29/30.	
30th	In trenches Souchez I	
31st	"	

Rhus Evans Captain for Lt Colonel
Comdg 1st Bn Worcestershire Regiment

1/5 Bn The Worcestershire Regiment

WAR DIARY
or
INTELLIGENCE SUMMARY.

Army Form C. 2118.

(Erase heading not required.)

Hour, Date, Place	Summary of Events and Information	Remarks and references to Appendices
1st April	In Right Bn of SOUCHEZ I Sector - weather fine and warm air fights. Hostile aircraft most active and seemed to be also active. Bombs were witnessed.	1 Sgt and 2 men killed. Stokes gun on the 3½" mortar was buried in a dart dump which caught fire and the lot blew up.
2nd	In same trenches. During the relief of the battn on the night 2/3rd the enemy violently bombarded the trenches and road and area behind. The bombardment was most intense and lasted from 8 Pm - 9 Pm at odd intervals. It is believed a relief was suspected of being carried out. Seven men of 2.E Lancs R.I. Rt. were wounded.	2 men wounded
3rd	On Billets at BOUVIGNY - weather fine and warm - working parties supplied night 3/4th - weather fine above trenches - working parties. - weather cold and cloudy	
4th	" " Relieved the 2 E Lancs in SOUCHEZ I.	Killed 1 man
5th	" "	
6th	Sector.	
7th	In above trenches - Trenches badly knocked in about - weather fine	
8th	" " weather fine	
9	" " weather that and	
10th	Col. Malone Fumbs - Enemy quiet - No trench mortaring weather wet	3 men killed, 3 men wounded
11th	" "	1 man killed

Army Form C. 2118.

WAR DIARY
or
INTELLIGENCE SUMMARY.
(Erase heading not required.)

Instructions regarding War Diaries and Intelligence Summaries are contained in F.S. Regs., Part II. and the Staff Manual respectively. Title pages will be prepared in manuscript.

Hour, Date, Place	Summary of Events and Information	Remarks and references to Appendices
12th April	In above trenches - Enemy quiet - Weather hot and cold. Relieved during the night 12/13th by the 2 E Lanc Regt and returned to trenches at BOIS DE NOULETTE HUTS.	
13th "	In above Billets - Working Parties supplied.	
14th "	"	4 men wounded on working party.
15th "	"	
16th "		
17th "	Relieved by 2.3rd R. Fusiliers 99th Bde - Bn on relief marched to billets at COUPIGNY.	
18th "	Moved to billets at BRUAY.	
19th "	In above billets - Company training - working parties	
20th "	"	
21st "	Weather wet.	
22nd "	In above billets - Good - Friday - weather hot and cold. working parties	
23rd "	Easter Sunday. The Sgts of the 2nd Bn came over from BETHUNE to play our Sgts. score 1-0 for the 2nd Bn: weather fine and warm.	

(73989) W4141—463. 400,000. 9/14. H.&J.Ltd. Forms/C. 2118/16.

Army Form C. 2118.

WAR DIARY
or
INTELLIGENCE SUMMARY.
(Erase heading not required.)

Instructions regarding War Diaries and Intelligence Summaries are contained in F. S. Regs., Part II. and the Staff Manual respectively. Title pages will be prepared in manuscript.

Hour, Date, Place	Summary of Events and Information	Remarks and references to Appendices
24th	Same biluets - working Parties. weather fine	
25th	— " — 7th Bn: Soccer team played the 25th Bn:	
26th	Regt: Game at BRUAY. Score 1-0 for the 1st Bn. working parties. weather fine.	
27th	Marched from BRUAY to BEAUMETZ (about 18 mls.) The march was very strenuous on the men as it was a fairly hot day. 7th Bn: left BRUAY at 8.20 am halted for 2 hours for dinner at FIEFS and arrived in new billets at 6 P.m. —	
27th	Started a weeks training in the manoeuvre area round BEAUMETZ. 1st day was given up to training weather fine and warm – fields good.	
28th	2nd Day. Company training – weather fine.	
29th	1st Day of Bn: training – weather fine and warm.	
30th	2nd Day of Bn: training. – weather fine and warm.	

30/11/16 ___ ___ 1st Bn ___ ___ Regt.

23

10th Bn Worcester Regt

WAR DIARY
or
INTELLIGENCE SUMMARY

Army Form C. 2118.

h 76 field May 1916. VK 18

(Erase heading not required.)

Place	Date	Hour	Summary of Events and Information	Remarks and references to Appendices
BRUAY ETZ	May 1st		Bn: Training from 9 am - 3.30 Pm	
-,-	2nd		" " "	
-,-	3rd		" " "	
-,-	4th		Cleaning up and preparing to move on the 5th inst.	
-,-	5th		Marched off at 7.20 am for PERNES. entrained at PERNES for HERSIN at 12.30 Pm arrived betw. plann at 3 Pm - Billets in HERSIN in THE CONVENT fields good.	
HERSIN	6th		Working parties of 300 men employed at ROUVIGNY – MIX-MAISETTE.	
-,-	7th		and 1 Pm and 3 - 4 Pm about 150 shells being fired in all - a few buildings damaged adj. weather fine. HERSIN shelled between 12 2am	
-,-	8th		Bn: Inspected by G.O.C. 23rd Division in Cl Square – working parties as usual – weather fine.	
-,-	9th		Hostile shelling about 50 shells put over no damage done – working parties as usual, weather fine	
-,-	10th		Relief of 2 R BERKS kept on tonight 10/11th in trenches I sector	

WAR DIARY or INTELLIGENCE SUMMARY.

Army Form C. 2118.

(Erase heading not required.)

Place	Date	Hour	Summary of Events and Information	Remarks and references to Appendices
Bouvigny	11th		relief completed by midnight. Order in trenches - B Coy right front. C Coy left front - 2 Platoons of each in front line, 2 in Support. - D Coy 2 Platoons SOUCHEZ Str. 2 Platoon HQ trench - A Coy Souchez Road - 6 Lewis guns in front line.	
"	12th		Little shelling or hostile sniping - no casualties. Trenches still very bad, very little work having been done on them since last Tuesday - men in them to trouble - Enemy quiet - work done on wire and deepening trenches.	2 Wounded
"	13th		"	1 Wounded
"	14th		"	1 "
"	15th		Relieved by 2/E Lancs Regt. relief completed by midnight. Relieved 9 pm - 10 pm a British attack took place on our right. VIMY RIDGE in which 2500 yds of trench were captured. Returned to billets in BOUVIGNY VILLAGE.	3 "
Bouvigny	16th		Billets BOUVIGNY. a bath. O.9.2. spent in front of village was being shelled the whole day - hostile fire of 200 men hostile fire & known	1 Wounded
"	17		Working parties 200 men hostile fire and known	

T2134. Wt. W708—776. 500000. 4/15. Sir J. C. & S.

Army Form C. 2118.

WAR DIARY
or
INTELLIGENCE SUMMARY.
(Erase heading not required.)

Place	Date	Hour	Summary of Events and Information	Remarks and references to Appendices
BOUVIGNY	18		Reliefs in BOUVIGNY - working parties 200 men breezte woven + fins	
-,-	19			
-,-	20		Relieved the 47th Division in BOUVIGNY HUTS on N-DAME-DE-LORETTE about 4.30 P.m. new billets quite good -	
BOUVIGNY HUTS	21		Above billets - A great deal of hostile shelling of battalion near billets 7.8" a number of splinters flying about - working party of 300 men in above billets - great deal of hostile shelters -	1 WOUNDED
-,-	22		Relief of 2nd Division - working party 250 men - weather fine + breeze - counter attack on VIMY	
-,-	23		In above billets - weather hot - lee lottes shelling town round working parties 250 men.	
-,-	24		In above Reliefs - working parties 200 men weather hot and windy so much hostile shelling in above Reliefs.	
-,-	25		working parties 200 men - weather fine	
-,-	26		working parties 200 men weather fine	
-,-	27		,,	
	28		,,	

Army Form C. 2118.

WAR DIARY
or
INTELLIGENCE SUMMARY.
(Erase heading not required.)

Place	Date	Hour	Summary of Events and Information	Remarks and references to Appendices
BOUVIGNY HUTS	29			
"	30		Working party of 200 men - weather wet. Left at one "hills" at 12 noon - daylight relief in ANGRES II. Relief relieving the 8 YORKS REGT. Our losses very good.	
ANGRES II	31		Holding ANGRES II sector	

31/5/16
F.C. Roberts. Captain acting for Colonel
Comdg 10th Bn Worcestershire Regt.

WAR DIARY or INTELLIGENCE SUMMARY

1 Worcester Regt
In the Field 1916
Army Form C. 2118.

Place	Date	Hour	Summary of Events and Information	Remarks and references to Appendices
	June			
ANGRES	1st		Considerable rifle grenade & Trench mortar activity each day. Trench artillery activity on both sides. Trenches shelled with howitzers at different times each day. Little damage. Much work done by night repairing trenches & erecting wire. Nightly patrols found enemy very quiet except for occasional bursts of M.G. fire at working parties. Enemy doing very little work on his front line. Two enemy patrols seen. Wrecks from which wiring.	3 Wounded
	2nd			4 — —
	3rd			6 — —
	4th		Relieved on 4th by day by 2nd E. Lancs. relief complete 2.30 p.m. moved into billets Fosse 10.	
FOSSE 10	5th to 9th		Very quiet. Billets good. Occasional rain. Working parties nightly in trenches.	
	10th		4 p.m. on 9th relieved 2nd E. Lancs in Angres II. 1 Coy R.W.R. (R.W.K.) attached for instruction 1 Platoon to each Coy in hills as before — 1 Coy Front line each 1 Platoon in support, 1 Coy in Reserve. Very quiet & uneventful tour	11th 3 Wounded B.D.
ANGRES II	11th 12th		Rifle grenade & trench mortar activity each day. Some heavy shells in hills. Little damage. Work on line & wire each night. Patrols found enemy very quiet. Rained every day. Much mud.	19.W 4 wounded

WAR DIARY
or
INTELLIGENCE SUMMARY.
(Erase heading not required.)

Army Form C. 2118.

Place	Date	Hour	Summary of Events and Information	Remarks and references to Appendices
ANGRES	11th		Morning of 11th Coy of R.M.C. took over section of front line from D Coy who proceeded into billets at Paum in Cellar. A Coy R.M.C. entered trenches relieved B Coy in Reserve who went into billets. Still raining.	
FOSSE 10	12th		A.T. Coy & C. Coy R.M.C. relieved by 19th London Regt. Relief complete 6pm. 12 Coy + H.Q. proceeded to billets at Fosse 10 for the night.	
FOSSE 10	13th		Marched off 8 am via Hersin Barlin Hordain to DIÉVAL. Arrived 1.30pm. Rained all the way. Billets good.	
DIÉVAL				
FIEFS	14th		Marched # at 9.15 am. via Pernes - Anich Ferme to FIEFS. Arrived 1.30pm. Officers billets indifferent.	
	15th		Remained in Bivfs. Resting, cleaning.	
FLECHIN	16th		Marched 8.30 am to Manouvers Area. Billets good but scattered. A.Q. A + D Coy Flechin B Coy Pippemont C Boncourt. Marches better - no rain.	
	17th		Bde training a manouver ground in vicinity of Boury - weather cold and dull.	
	18th		Training under Bn: arrangement in open order fighting etc - weather cold and dull.	

Army Form C. 2118.

WAR DIARY
or
INTELLIGENCE SUMMARY.
(Erase heading not required.)

Place	Date	Hour	Summary of Events and Information	Remarks and references to Appendices
FLEABIN	19		Training – a Divisional day. – Practice in to behave in a position – consolidate a position won and intercommunication between HQ and aeroplane. Weather cold and dull.	
—	20		Training under Bn. arrangements. – To assault a flour river and wood fighting practised – weather dull	
—	21		Training under Bn. arrangements – Draft of 27 o'Ranks – healthy fair.	
—	22		Training under Coy arrangements – weather very fine and warm	
—	23		Training under Coy arrangements in hills. Weather warm	
—	24		Marched from FLEABIN at 9 am reached LILLERS 12·30 pm entrained at 2·30 pm for LONGUEAU near AMIENS arriving at 9·30 pm detrained and marched to billets in ST SAUVEUR about 5 miles W of AMIENS arrived in billets 4 AM on 25th. – weather warm	
ST-SAUVEUR	25		Billets fairly good but rather crowded. weather wet	
—	26		"			2 above billets. Coy inspections weather wet and warm	
—	27		"			Coy training weather wet.	

Army Form C. 2118.

WAR DIARY
or
INTELLIGENCE SUMMARY.
(Erase heading not required.)

Instructions regarding War Diaries and Intelligence Summaries are contained in F. S. Regs., Part II. and the Staff Manual respectively. Title pages will be prepared in manuscript.

Place	Date	Hour	Summary of Events and Information	Remarks and references to Appendices
ST SAUVEUR	28		recvd. some kilts - Coy training - weather hot.	
"	29		" " " "	
"	30		Left billets during the evening for Clair killed at RAINNEVILLE about 7 miles NE of AMIENS.	

W. Robt. K. Leslie Capt & to L. Colonel
30/6 Comdg 1/8 Bn Lancashire Yorkshire Regiment

24th Inf.Bde.
8th Div.

Battn. with Brigade
rejoined 8th Div.
from 23rd Div. III.
Corps, 15.7.16.

WAR DIARY

1st BATTN. THE WORCESTERSHIRE REGIMENT.

J U L Y

1 9 1 6

Army Form C. 2118

1st Worcestershire Regiment

WAR DIARY
or
INTELLIGENCE SUMMARY.
(Erase heading not required.)

July 1916   Vol 20

Place	Date	Hour	Summary of Events and Information	Remarks and references to Appendices
MOLLIENS-AU-BOIS	1st July		Arrived in close billets MOLLIENS-AU-BOIS about 9.30 PM the night of the 30th June. Three Bdes of the Bdry billeted in same Village. Accommodation very limited – weather fine and warm – Removal in which MOLLIENS-AU-BOIS until 6 PM at which time orders were received to be ready to move in one hour's time – Left at 9 PM and marched to HENENCOURT and billeted in huts in HENENCOURT WOOD arrived at HENENCOURT about 2.30 AM	
	2nd		Billeted in HENENCOURT WOOD – weather fine and warm.	
	3rd		– weather wet	
	4th		Left HENENCOURT at 6 AM and marched in a Bde to billets of DERNANCOURT – close fields – weather wet. Billeted in DERNANCOURT – weather very wet.	
	5th		Reconnoitred route to FRICOURT and BECOURT WOOD – Left DERNANCOURT at 8.30 PM – In the evening the Battalion bivouacked for 2 hours WEST OF FRICOURT, moving off at 6.45 PM preparatory to active operations on the morning July 5th	

WAR DIARY or INTELLIGENCE SUMMARY

Army Form C. 2118

Place	Date	Hour	Summary of Events and Information	Remarks and references to Appendices
FRICOURT	1st		Orders for a Bde attack were received in the early morning. The general idea being as follows:- Contingent on the success of a night attack by the 62nd Bde on PEARL ALLEY and QUADRANGLE support trenches, the 1st Worcestershires were to occupy trench junction, leaving portion's north of & SHELTER Trench and SHELTER ALLEY to 5th Battalion of PEARL ALLEY and SHELTER ALLEY. Then at 8 am, the Battalion was in due course directed to attack CONTALMAISON in two lines. PEARL ALLEY — CONTALMAISON CHURCH — CHATEAU, subject to a bombardment of our artillery on CONTALMAISON between 7 am – 8 am & 9/10 am attacking CONTALMAISON on our left from PEARE WOOD at the same time (8 am). In the course of the night 6/7 the battalion (Worcesters) had gained the following positions B and C Coys under Lieut. H. JAMES V.C. and Captain A.B. PRATT respectively, SHELTER ALLEY to junction of PEARL ALLEY. D Coy Captain WILKINS SHELTER TRENCH. A Coy Captain J.R.L. EVANS CRUCIFIX TRENCH. In the meantime the night attack of the 62nd Bde had failed and about 4 am the Germans delivered a counter attack against it from the direction of PEARL ALLEY & on the front of C Coy who was able to materially assist in repulsing the counter attack — in the meantime orders were received to hold an gun attack on CONTALMAISON. About 8 am our artillery as a report of a German counterattack from QUADRANGLE SUPPORT, subsequently proved to be false, our guns opened an intense barrage on PEARL Alley & sv Trench and NORTH end of SHELTER	

WAR DIARY or INTELLIGENCE SUMMARY

Army Form C. 2118

Place	Date	Hour	Summary of Events and Information	Remarks and references to Appendices
BECOURT	7/7/16		Trenches - Many shells fell in our vicinity this, causing casualties in B & C Coy, and compelled "C" Coy to evacuate a low portion of SHELTER ALLEY. B Coy & the meanwhile working N NORTH of PEARL ALLEY along SHELTER Trench; in order to notify our adv. that they were falling a us and not on the enemy, many very heavy shots of B and C Coy without known our effect. Between 9 am - 10 am PEARL ALLEY fell into the hands of the 52 Bde, and reports being received from Willing observer that BAILIFF WOOD and Northern portion of CONTALMAISON were held by our troops. Orders were received by us that we proceed with the attack, a confirmation from the South. These apply chiefly found to be entirely false and misleading - At about 10:30 am B Coy at once attacked and relieved CONTALMAISON returning as far as THE CHURCH, and taking a number of prisoners (about 75). I hear they looted from the cellars in CONTALMAISON - The advance was made along the SUNKEN ROAD and 60 YARDS WEST of it - C Coy got into junction about an hour later working their way in on the right of B Coy. Fierce hand to hand fighting ensuing. Then the Germans held an better position in CONTALMAISON till about 2 P.m. D Coy coming of School trench Suffet about 1Pm endeavoured to work its way into the village from within flank a Nth side of the WOOD - In Coy	

Army Form C. 2118

WAR DIARY
or
INTELLIGENCE SUMMARY.
(Erase heading not required.)

Place	Date	Hour	Summary of Events and Information	Remarks and references to Appendices
FRICOURT	7th		Meanwhile the retirement of the 2/E Yorks Regt from PEAKE WOOD failed in its objects as it came under heavy m.gun fire from PEAKE WOOD. The Germans in the meanwhile held the northern portion of the village and though at 1.30 P.M. D Coy was still in the vicinity of the Iron Cross and within 300 yards thereof, before our front line a counter-attack could be secured the Germans maintained a strong counter-attack through BOTTOM and QUADRANGLE on our right flank supported by m.gun fire which swept both our flanks from BAILIFF WOOD and that portion of QUADRANGLE Trench which runs from PEARL ALLEY to THE CUTTING. In the meanwhile at last our forces impossible to get A Coy s/n back to retrieve the position, as the attack broke, and the train came down to ground. Shooting communication trenches, and recovering to ground suffering and with informants many steady reinforcement. — The remnants of those circumstances were that the Germans from 2 P.M. onward, assisted by heavy shell fire, beat us back. Though cut off at CONTAY MAISON, the battalion having been quite surrounded had heavy losses and by 5 P.M. battalion was back in SHELTER ALLEY, from where to CONTAY MAISON and Cub into it, SOUTHWARD to PEARL ALLEY and SHELTER WOOD — By 8 P.M. D and A Coys were left-field working, finishing in SHELTER ALLEY and B & C Coys	

WAR DIARY or INTELLIGENCE SUMMARY

Army Form C. 2118

Place	Date	Hour	Summary of Events and Information	Remarks and references to Appendices
FRICOURT	7th		withdrawn to the vicinity of CRUCIFIX TRENCH. — Our failure to make good CONFIRMATION was felt to be for the following reasons. (1) Change of original Programme. (2) Losses and shaking received by B & C Coy in their dash from our own artillery barrage which upset the previously arranged continuation of thus the Companies of completing C Coy's withdrawal down SHELTER ALLEY. (3) The fact that when the battalion did advance it found itself unsupported & organized for BAZENTIF WOOD, and the burnt remnants of the artillery which greatly facilitated the task of the counter attack. (4) The failure of the Left attack (2 E Lancer Regt) from PEAKE WOOD to make good the northern portion of the trench. Great support of the it had talked CONFIRMATION.	
			(5) The weather condition. Had the Tornados not broken ½ minute before the attack of G.75.2. halts old wires seen by us might have matched A Coy and some scattered portions of G.75.2. and made good our position in CONTALMAISON.	
FRICOURT	8th		During the forenoon and afternoon of the 8th a strong reconnaissance under Captain LITTLE of D Coy was pushed up to CONTALMAISON and found it strongly held by the enemy. At 4.45 PM an order was received from 24th Bde that our attack CONTALMAISON, artillery observers having reported our troops as having entered the village from the WEST. These reports were quite false and not in accordance with information gained	

WAR DIARY or INTELLIGENCE SUMMARY

Army Form C. 2118

Place	Date	Hour	Summary of Events and Information	Remarks and references to Appendices
FRICOURT	8th		Four battns - At about 5.30 P.m. the battalion was getting into position to attack from PEARL ALLEY, in conjunction with the 2nd Northants Regt. who were already deployed for the attack from the direction of PEAKE WOOD. At this hour the enemy opened a tremendous barrage on all troops/roads leading from SHELTER ALLEY to PEAKE WOOD and as far down as SHELTER WOOD, at which point was SHELTER ALLEY communication run NORTH - The 2nd Northants Regt. appeared to be caught in their barrage whilst in the act of deploying, and soon began to fall back and by 6.30 P.m. were in their original position. In the meanwhile the battn: with some losses had worked forward along SHELTER TRENCH, NORTH of PEARL ALLEY, and there awaited orders as regards attacking - Since the advance of 2nd Northants Regt. being a total failure, instructions laid down for the attack no longer availed. - At 7 P.m. orders were received from 24th & 73rd Bdes. not to attack and to withdraw the companies to CRUCIFIX TRENCH, and that the companies on before along SHELTER ALLEY. - This movement was accordingly completed by 8 P.m. A & C Coys remain in SHELTER trench.	
FRICOURT	9th		During the whole of the day no P.m. remained on above - In the evening of A and C Coys were relieved by 2 companies of the 10th W RIDING Regt 68 Bdy and the sent for: HQ	

WAR DIARY or INTELLIGENCE SUMMARY.

Army Form C. 2118

Place	Date	Hour	Summary of Events and Information	Remarks and references to Appendices
PRICOURT	9th		Withdrew to LOZENGE WOOD	2/Lt Carruthers from B. to F. 10th
-:-	10th		During to-day the 10th W.R. was in reserve in LOZENGE WOOD and was relieved in all its positions about 9 pm by the 10th GLOSTER REGt and marched to billets at BRESLE -	Officers Killed Wounded 5 8
BRESLE	11th		In billets at BRESLE. Left at 6 pm for MOULLIENS-AU-BOIS arriving soon after 10 pm - billeted for the night.	O.R.s Killed Wounded 25 235
MOULLIENS AU Bois	12th		Left MOULLIENS-AU-BOIS by 10 am and marched to PIERREGOT about 2 kilos distance - billeted for the night. 12/13	missing 44
PIERREGOT	13th		Left PIERREGOT at 3 pm and marched to POULAINVILLE about 5½ miles, billeted for the night.	
POULAINVILLE	14th		Left POULAINVILLE at 10 pm and marched to LONGUEAU close to AMIENS where he Battn entrained for BETHUNE arriving about midnight 14/15	24th Bdo rejoined the 8th Division
FOUGUEREUIL	15th		Billeted in villages of FOUGUEREUIL about 2 miles from BETHUNE. I rejoined the 8th Division billets at Mr.	
-:-	16		Inspection of Batts. by Divisn - Cleaning up - weather wet.	
	17		Billeted as above - Inspection by G.O.C. 8th Divisn - weather wet.	

Army Form C. 2118.

WAR DIARY
or
INTELLIGENCE SUMMARY.
(Erase heading not required.)

Instructions regarding War Diaries and Intelligence Summaries are contained in F. S. Regs., Part II. and the Staff Manual respectively. Title pages will be prepared in manuscript.

Place	Date	Hour	Summary of Events and Information	Remarks and references to Appendices
FOUQUEREUIL	18		In close billets - weather hot	
-"-	19		" "	
-"-	20		2y I Bdg inspected by General Munro Commanding 1st Army - weather fine	
-"-	21		Billets as above - weather fine	
-"-	22		Road at 9am to BEVRY - Billets very good - Bring in Divisional Reserve Weather dull.	
BEVRY	23		Same billets - Company training - weather dull	
-"-	24		Mixed Draft of Oxford & Bucks, Gloucester, and Berks joined Bn to the strength of 350. - weather dull	
-"-	25		Same billets - weather dull -	
-"-	26		" Coy training	
-"-	27		" weather fine - Coy training.	
-"-	28		" "	
-"-	29		" "	
-"-	30		Relieved 2d Welsh Regt in CUINCHY SECTOR - Relief complete 9.40pm - Trenches fair - weather fine	
-"-	31		In above trenches - weather fine and warm. -	

31th Coy by 5th Worcestershire Regt Lt Colonel

8th, Division.

24th, Brigade.

1st, Worcester Regt.

Augus t, 1916.

WAR DIARY
or
INTELLIGENCE SUMMARY.
(Erase heading not required.)

Army Form C. 2118

B.D. N/8
1st Bn Worcestershire Regiment
Aug 1915

Vol 21

Place	Date	Hour	Summary of Events and Information	Remarks and references to Appendices
				Casualties
				Killed / Wounded
CUINCHY TRENCHES	1st Aug		Bn holding CUINCHY trenches from BOYAU to the LA BASSÉE CANAL — Weather very fine — a great deal of hostile trench mortaring	4 / 4
"	2nd Aug		Holding trenches. Weather fine — Very quiet day — hostile trench mortaring at night	— / 1
"	3rd Aug		" "	— / 1
"	4th "		" "	— / —
"	5th "		Relieved during the afternoon by the 5/6 Royal Scots Regt — Marched to billets in BETHUNE — billets good —	— / 1
BILLETS	6th		1st Army Church Parade in GRANDE PLACE BETHUNE to commemorate 2 years war — weather fine and warm.	
"	7th		Enemy heavily shelled BETHUNE doing much damage	1 / 3
"	8th		In billets as above weather finer	
"	9th		Took over trenches from 2nd Devons (QUARR. SECTION)	1 / 5
TRENCHES	10th		A.B.D Coys front line. C Coy support	
"	10th		Holding trenches — Hostile Trench Mortars fairly active	1 / 2
"	11th		Do. Very quiet during day — weather fine	1 / 3
"	12th		A.B.C. Coys relieved by 2/Northants. D Coy remaining in front line	

H.W.
Extract

Army Form C. 2118

WAR DIARY
or
INTELLIGENCE SUMMARY.
(Erase heading not required.)

Instructions regarding War Diaries and Intelligence Summaries are contained in F.S. Regs., Part II. and the Staff Manual respectively. Title pages will be prepared in manuscript.

Place	Date	Hour	Summary of Events and Information	Remarks and references to Appendices
TRENCHES	12/6			Casualties KILLED-W.D 3 /16 2/Lt Fisher Wounded 1 "Baker"
"	13"	8 pm	A.B.D.C Coys moved back into Support. Enemy violent trenches on our left held by W.YORKS after very heavy bombardment which extended our front held by D Coy	
"	14"		D Coy relieved by C Coy - shelled heavily during the afternoon - Batn holding same position - intermittent shelling	
"	15"		Relieved by 1st R.I.R. about 6 pm - marched back to billets at FOUQUEREUIL - billets very good	1
BILLETS	16"		In billets - inspection of clothing etc Supplies working parties under R.E.	
"	17"		do	
"	18"		do	
"	19"		do Drill parades during morning Church Parade service by assistant Chaplain General (Revd Blackburn) at FOUQUIERES	
"	20"		In billets - Coy commanders visited trenches prior to taking over - 14 o/r O's joined Bn from England -	
"	21"		" " " - similar number to the sent back to explain them	

Army Form C.

WAR DIARY
or
INTELLIGENCE SUMMARY.
(Erase heading not required.)

Instructions regarding War Diaries and Intelligence Summaries are contained in F.S. Regs., Part II. and the Staff Manual respectively. Title pages will be prepared in manuscript.

Place	Date	Hour	Summary of Events and Information	Remarks and references to Appendices
BILLETS	22/7		In billets. Party of 14 NCOs to England	Casualties KD - WD
"	23/7		Took over trenches (HOHENZOLLERN SECTION) from 2nd Devons	
TRENCHES	24/7		about 3 P.M. - quiet - relief - A.B.C. Coys front line, Day Support about	2
"	25/7		Holding trenches. Hostile T.M's fairly active - weather fine - fairly quiet	5
"	26/7		do	2
"	27/7		do - Front line badly damaged by enemy shell fire	3
"	28/7		Relieved by 2/E.LANCS about 10 am - Front line trenches in this sector very bad - Bn moved back into "Support" Bn in support of trenches - weather fair	
"	29/7		do - weather heavy thunder storms	
"	30/7		do - weathered very unsettled	
"	31/7		Took over front line trenches from 2/E.LANCS about 11am A.C.D Coys in front line, B Coy in support	

Commdg. 1st Bn Worcestershire Regt.
Wm L Colonel

8th, Division.

24th, Brigade.

1st, Bn Worcester Regt.

September, 1916.

Army Form C. 2118.

Vol 2. 1st Bn Worcestershire Regt

WAR DIARY
or
INTELLIGENCE SUMMARY.
(Erase heading not required.)

Instructions regarding War Diaries and Intelligence Summaries are contained in F. S. Regs., Part II. and the Staff Manual respectively. Title pages will be prepared in manuscript.

Place	Date	Hour	Summary of Events and Information	Remarks and references to Appendices
				Casualties
				KD / WD
France	1/10		Holding front line trenches (HOHENZOLLERN SECTION) A C Coys in front line. A Coy in Support. Weather changeable	1 / 4
TRENCHES	2/10		Holding trenches as above. Enemy fairly quiet.	
"	3 "		do. slight increase in hostile T M activity.	1
"	4 "		do. Enemy fairly quiet; weather stormy	
"	5 "		Bn relieved in front line by 2/E Lancs about 3 pm. Battn took up position in reserve line from them, very wet. Battalion Hd Qrs in VERMELLES	2
"	6 "		do. weather improved but still some showers	
"	7 "		do	
"	8 "		do	
"	9 "		Bn employed finding working parties at night for bringing up R.E. stores.	x
"	9 "		Bn relieved by 2/R.BERKS about 4 pm. Marched back & took over billets from 2/RB. Relieving of LABOURSE billets very good. Bn proceeded to GOSNAY for instructional purposes at Div School of Instruction	2 L
BILLETS	10"		Instruction by O.C. Coys.	22.W 3 weeks
"	11"		Coys placed at disposal of O.C. Coys for drill etc.	

Army Form C. 2118.

WAR DIARY
or
INTELLIGENCE SUMMARY.
(Erase heading not required.)

Instructions regarding War Diaries and Intelligence Summaries are contained in F.S. Regs., Part II. and the Staff Manual respectively. Title pages will be prepared in manuscript.

Place	Date	Hour	Summary of Events and Information	Remarks and references to Appendices
				Casualties
				K.D. — W.O.
LABOURSE				
BILLETS	12/76		Bn in billets. Bn employed by O.C. weather fine	
—	13"		do — Drill & manoeuvre during morning	
—	14"		do — Employed fatigue parties carrying up R.A.T.S. to front line	
—	15"		do — Coys at drill etc under O.C Coys	
—	16"		do — O.C. Coys visited trenches (QUARRY SECTION)	
—	17"		Bn took over trenches (QUARRY SECTION) from 2/WYORKS about 5 P.m	1
			Bn occupied reserve line in front of VERMELLES	
TRENCHES	18"		Bn in reserve trenches	
—	19"		do — Supplied fatigue parties for front line etc	1
—	20"		do — Weather fine during period in reserve	
—	21"		Bn took over front line trenches from 1/8/FORESTERS. # B, C, D Coys in	1
			Front-line A Coy in reserve	
—	22"		Holding front-line trenches — enemy fairly quiet	
—	23"		— Hostile T.Ms very active doing considerable damage	5
—	24"		do — Sectors allotted to Bn front reversed. A Coy moved	2 3
			up to front line. Hostile T.M again very active	

T2134. Wt. W708—776. 500000. 4/16. Sir J.C.& S.

Army Form C. 2118.

WAR DIARY
or
INTELLIGENCE SUMMARY.
(Erase heading not required.)

Instructions regarding War Diaries and Intelligence Summaries are contained in F.S. Regs., Part II. and the Staff Manual respectively. Title pages will be prepared in manuscript.

Place	Date	Hour	Summary of Events and Information	Remarks and references to Appendices
TRENCHES	25/6		Enemy holding front line, continued activity by hostile Artillery & T.M. fire, doing considerable damage. (C.S.M. Solari killed)	Casualties KD — WD 3 4
— " —	26 "		Still holding front line, enemy still fairly active	2 2
— " —	27 "		do. enemy hot, such - so action so last few days	
— " —	28 "		do. enemy fairly quiet	3
— " —	29 "		On relieving in front line by 2/1E Lancs, took up position in reserve line in front of VERMELLES	
— " —	30 "		Enemy in Regtl Reserve in same trenches	

H. C. ? Lt Col
Comdg Worcestershire Regt

8th, Division.

24th, Brigade,

1st, Bn Worcester Regt.

October, 1916.

1st Worcestershire R.gt. 24/8
Army Form C. 2118.
Vol 23

J.D.
23.W
3 Mat

WAR DIARY
or
INTELLIGENCE SUMMARY
(Erase heading not required.)

October 1916

Place	Date	Hour	Summary of Events and Information	Remarks and references to Appendices
France	Oct			
	1st		In Support Trenches, Quarries Section, Hohenzollern. Weather Wet; Casualties Nil	
	2nd		As above, in support to 2nd E. Lancs. Weather Wet. Casualties Nil	
	3rd		Relieved 2nd East Lancs in front line. Weather Wet. Casualties Nil. Trenches in bad state	
	4th		As above. Trench Mortars active, indirect fire carried out. Casualties 2 O.R. wounded.	
	5th		As above. Quiet during day. Heavy hostile fire at night between hours of 8 p.m. and 11 a.m. Casualties 1 Officer & 1 Lieut. C.W.H. Mueller) killed 2 O.R. Mueller) killed 2 O.R. wounded. Weather changeable.	
	6th		Quiet during morning. Later in Trench Mortars & Artillery active (hostile) Casualties Wounded 2 O.R.	
	7th		Battalion relieved by 2nd East Lancs, & W. Midlows. to Support Trenches. Weather Wet.	
	8th		In support trenches. Taking up parties to front line. Weather fine	
	9th		As for 8th	
	10th		As above.	
	11th		Bn relieved by 2nd Bn. Yorks. Regt. & billets in LABOURSE.	
	12th		In billets. Rest and refitting & cleaning up.	
	13th		In billets. Preparations for move by train to South.	

Army Form C. 2118.

1st Worcestershire R. Jt.

WAR DIARY
or
INTELLIGENCE SUMMARY.
(Erase heading not required.)

Instructions regarding War Diaries and Intelligence Summaries are contained in F. S. Regs., Part II and the Staff Manual respectively. Title pages will be prepared in manuscript.

Place	Date	Hour	Summary of Events and Information	Remarks and references to Appendices
	Oct 14th		Battalion marched to FOUQUEREUIL 3 a.m. entrained, arrived and detrained at LONG PRE about 3 p.m. marched to CITE ANES. Took over billets at about 4 p.m. Weather fine.	
	15th		In billets. Weather fine. Orders received for move forward.	
	16th		Battalion marched to SOREL. Thence by motor omnibus to MEAULTE arrived at about 6 p.m. Marched to SANDPITS VALLEY camp. Under canvas. Weather fine.	
	17th		In above camp. Weather fine.	
	18th		In above camp. Weather fine.	
	19th		Bn. relieved 9/2 Norfolks. N.E. of GUEUDECOURT in SHINE & RAINBOW TRENCHES (under) from camp at 7 a.m. about 5 miles. Weather very wet, and going very bad indeed.	
	20th		In above trenches. Casualties 1 O.R. killed 6 O.R. wounded 1 O.R. missing, believed killed	
	21st		In above trenches. Casualties killed 11 O.R. Wounded 33 O.R. & 2 officers (Messrs J.O.R. believed killed) Enemy shelling very severe indeed and continuous.	
	22nd		Bn relieved by 1/F Lancs & 1 W.Ridrus to Needle Trench.	
	23rd		In Needle Trench. 2 Companies moved up to SHINE and Belfast Trenches in close support to 2/F. Lancs, who were attacking MILD TRENCH Casualties F.O.R. wounded.	
	24th		In Needle Trench as above. Wounded 6. O.R.	

Army Form C. 2118.

1st Worcestershire

WAR DIARY
or
INTELLIGENCE SUMMARY.

(Erase heading not required.)

Place	Date	Hour	Summary of Events and Information	Remarks and references to Appendices
	25R /0 J.T		Battalion relieved 2nd S. Lans in MILD & SHINE TRENCHES North East of GUEDECOURT. All P.'s in RAINBOW TRENCH Casualties 1.O.R. Killed 2.O.R. Wounded.	
	26R		In about trenches. Very severe shelling by enemy. Killed 2 O.R. wounded 9 O.R.	
	27R		In above trenches Wounded 6 O.R. Died of wounds 1 O.R.	
	28R		As above Wounded 34. O.R. Killed 9 O.R.	
	29R		As above Killed 1 O.R. Wounded 6 O.R.	
	30R		Bn relieved by West R. Rango 9th Bn about 10.30 p.m. Spent night at TROUNES WOOD. Weather very wet and going almost impossible	
	31st /3		Battalion Marched to SANDPITS bivouacking about 4 p.m. The Battalion had a very rough time in the gun trenches, no every is striking and was very intense, and trenches afforded little cover. The ground difficulty was found in the matter of supply as all ratios & water had to be brought up by pack animal & man handling. 5 or 6 miles over a sodden waste of shell holes, which in conjunction with the wet weather became a sticky morass wet mud.	

Major Capt & Adjt
Commanding, 1st Worcestershire Regt

8th, Division.

24th, Brigade.

Ist, Bn Worcester Regt.

November, 1916.

Army Form C. 2118

WAR DIARY
or
INTELLIGENCE SUMMARY.
(Erase heading not required.)

1/Worcesters   Nov. 1916

Place	Date	Hour	Summary of Events and Information	Remarks and references to Appendices
	Nov			
	1st		At Sandpit Camp — Draft arrived from Manchester Reg.	
	2nd		As above	
	3rd		As above	
	4th		As above	
	5th		Moved from Sandpit camp to Hut at Carnoy — very crowded	
	6th		Relieved 2/Worcesters Regt at Guillemont in Reserve	
	7th		In Reserve at Guillemont	
	8th		Relieved 2/Elses in trenches SE of Lesboeufs — left South — Right Brigade not to take	
	9th		Relieved by 2/Berks went to camp at Bridgoatlane — easy relief	
	10th		At Bryantine Camp	
	11th		As above	
	12th		As above	
	13th		As above. Left camp night of 13/14th for trenches near Les Boeufs relieved W. Yorkshire Regt. Enemy shelled Les Boeufs heavily	
	14th		In trenches — Les Boeufs	24 W
	15th		As above. 3rd line shelled heavily Killed 12 OR wounded 1 officer 12 OR relieved	2 w

Army Form C. 2118.

1 Worcester Regt
Vol 24

WAR DIARY
or
INTELLIGENCE SUMMARY.
(Erase heading not required.)

Instructions regarding War Diaries and Intelligence Summaries are contained in F.S. Regs., Part II. and the Staff Manual respectively. Title pages will be prepared in manuscript.

Place	Date	Hour	Summary of Events and Information	Remarks and references to Appendices
	Nov 15th		Relieved right of 15/16th by 2nd LANCASHIRE Regt. went into reserve line	
	16th		Reserve line FLERS. One Company in TRONES WOOD	
	17th		Relieved by 2nd HAMPSHIRE Regt and NEWFOUNDLAND Regt and marched to CARNOY CAMP (NORTH).	
	18th		Marched to billets in MEAULTE at 11.30 am - Billets fair.	
	19th		Billets in MEAULTE.	
	20th		Marched to EDGEHILL entrained and detrained at AIRAINES - train very late - marched to Billets in AUMONT. Billets good.	
	21st-24th		In Billets at AUMONT	
	25th		As above	
	26th		As above Church Parade	
	27th		As above Draft of 12 O.Rs	
	28th		As above	
	29th		As above Draft of 2 O.Rs	
	30th		As above	

8th, Division.

24th, Brigade,

1st, Bn Worcester Regt.

December, 1916.

Army Form C. 2118.

1/7 WORCESTERSHIRE R
WAR DIARY
or
INTELLIGENCE SUMMARY.
(Erase heading not required.)

Vol 2 5

Place	Date	Hour	Summary of Events and Information	Remarks and references to Appendices
AUMONT	Sept 1st		Training of Companies in attack formation + musketry	Weather mostly dull
			Lewis Gunners & Snipers + lnd shots of Batt. on range	
	2nd		Route march (Bgde Cross Country run)	
	3rd		Divine Service	
	4th		Training of Companies under O.C. Coy arrangements	
	5th		"	
	6th		"	
	7th		"	Marshal Chougarde
	8th		"	
	9th		Route March - 3rd Cross Country Run	Rain + Snow
	10th		Divine Service	
	11th		Practice advance of successive waves to an attack under creeping barrage coloured flags being used to represent barrage	
	12th		ditto	
	13th		Practice cooperation of Lewis Gunners + Mortars in trench attack	25 W 4m

1st WORCESTERSHIRE R

Army Form C. 2118.

WAR DIARY
or
INTELLIGENCE SUMMARY.
(Erase heading not required.)

Place	Date	Hour	Summary of Events and Information	Remarks and references to Appendices
AU MONT het				
	15th		Instruction by R.E.'s on rapid wiring by day & night	
	16		ditto	
	"		Use of bangalore torpedo. Theoretical & practical. Bangalore torpedo exploded to blow a gap in wire. Bombers attack trench through gap	
	17th		Brown Service. Weather wet & cold	
	18th		Battalion in attack on trenches in various formations using flags to represent creeping barrage.	
	19th		ditto	
	20th		"	
	21st		"	
	22nd		Route march.	
	23rd		Brown Service	
	24th		Xmas Day. Divine Service.	
	25th			
	26th		Company training	

Army Form C. 2118.

1ST WORCESTER REGT

WAR DIARY
or
INTELLIGENCE SUMMARY.
(Erase heading not required.)

Place	Date	Hour	Summary of Events and Information	Remarks and references to Appendices
AUMONT	27		Battalion training	
"	28		Inspection by G.O.C. 5th Division.	
"	29		Entrained at AIRAINES detrained EDGEHILL marched to No 112 Camp situate on the MEAULTE-BRAY Road.	
"	30		Moved to No 16 Camp situate on the BRAY-MARICOURT Road. Camp in very dirty condition. Draft of eight O.Ranks arrived.	
"	31		Cleaning up camp.	

WAR DIARY 1st Bn. WORCESTERSHIRE Regt.
or
INTELLIGENCE SUMMARY.

Army Form C. 2118

Vol 26

Place	Date	Hour	Summary of Events and Information	Remarks and references to Appendices
In the field	1/1/17		Battalion in Camp No 16 very wet and cold (cleaning and drawing Camp).	
	2		do	
	3		do	
	4		do	
	5		do	
	6		do	
	7		do	
	8		do	Draft of 1 Officer 25 O/Ranks.
	9		Marched to VAUX 16 billets - Billets fair.	
	10		In Billets at VAUX.	
	11		Marched to MÉRICOURT L'ABBÉ entrained and detrained at AIRAINES. Marched to Billets at VERGIES. Billets good.	
	12		Cleaning up.	
	13		Battalion Training in new Attack formations, Specialists, bombing etc. G.O.C. 5th Div. visited VERGIES. Battle Patrol Platoon inaugurated.	
	14		Training as above.	

WAR DIARY
or
INTELLIGENCE SUMMARY.
(Erase heading not required.)

Army Form C. 2118

Place	Date	Hour	Summary of Events and Information	Remarks and references to Appendices
In the field	Jan 15		Battalion in training	
	16		do	
	17		do	
	18		Battalion inspected by Brigadier General Cotham DSO G.O.C 74 th Infantry Bgde. in training. Brigadier's Conference.	
	19		" " G.O.C. 8th Division inspected Battle Battn. Platoon.	
	20		" "	
	21		" "	
	22		" Marched to BOISEMENT entrained and detrained at EDGEHILL	
	23		Marched to Camp No 13, on the MORLANCOURT - CHIPILLY Road	
	24		At Camp No 13.	
	25		do	
	26		Bn marched to Camp No 21 on the HARICOURT - SOUSANNE Rd	
			" paraded for trenches 1.15 PM, took over from the 14th Bn Argyle & Sutherland Highlanders in the BOUCHAVESNES NORTH Sector Relief complete 7.35 PM.	
	27		Enemy Quiet	Casualties 1 OR killed
	28		Normal	2 -- wounded

Army Form C. 2118.

WAR DIARY
or
INTELLIGENCE SUMMARY.
(Erase heading not required.)

Instructions regarding War Diaries and Intelligence Summaries are contained in F. S. Regs., Part II. and the Staff Manual respectively. Title pages will be prepared in manuscript.

Place	Date	Hour	Summary of Events and Information	Remarks and references to Appendices
In trifles	29		BOUCHAVESNE 9th NORTH Sector – Normal	
	30		Normal.	
	31		Normal.	

WAR DIARY 1st Bn. The Worcestershire Regt. Army Form C. 2118.
or
INTELLIGENCE SUMMARY.

Ref. ALBERT. Continued Sheet.

Place	Date	Hour	Summary of Events and Information	Remarks and references to Appendices
In the Field	1st Feb.		In Trenches. BOUCHAVESNES N. Sector. Very Cold Weather. Casualties 3 O.R. Wounded	
	2nd		As above	
	3rd		Relieved at 9 p.m. by 2nd E Lancashire Regt and went back to ASQUITHS FLATS (B 23 b.4.7) Brigade Reserve.	
	4th		Brigade Reserve. 1 O.R. wounded whilst on working party.	
	5th	- do -	Draft of 1 Offr. and 14 O.R. joined	
	6th	- do -	Casualties 2 O.R. wounded.	
	7/9	- do -		
	10'	-	Relieved at 3.45 pm by 1st Household Bn, embussed at CRUCIFIX CORNER (B14.a.9.4) and proceeded to Camp No.124 on the S. side of the SAILLY LE SEC - SAILLY LAURETTE Road (T 35 l. 34). Very good camp, but left in bad condition.	
	11/20		At Camp No.124. Bn in training for attack on FRITZ Trench. new formation adopted also picture Trenches of Objective, and our own lines used. During the latter days of Training, the attack in detail was carried out. The Bn also assembled for attack in the dark. Battle Patrol Platoon practised raid on BREMEN TRENCH. Training of Specialists was also given great attention.	

Army Form C. 2118.

WAR DIARY
or
INTELLIGENCE SUMMARY.
(Erase heading not required.)

Instructions regarding War Diaries and Intelligence Summaries are contained in F. S. Regs., Part II. and the Staff Manual respectively. Title pages will be prepared in manuscript.

Place	Date	Hour	Summary of Events and Information	Remarks and references to Appendices
	22 Feb		Moved from Camp 124 to billets in BRAY. Close billets. These were left in dirty condition.	
	23/24		Billetted in BRAY.	
	25/27		Moved to VAUX. Training continued. Assembly for attack in dark.	
	28	-	Moved to BRAY. Billetted there in Billets in dirty condition.	

A. B. Pratt
CAPTAIN.
ADJUTANT 1st BN. THE WORCESTERSHIRE REGIMENT.

WAR DIARY or INTELLIGENCE SUMMARY

Army Form C. 2118.

1st Bn the Worcestershire Regiment

Vol 28

Place	Date	Hour	Summary of Events and Information	Remarks and references to Appendices
	1917			
BRAY	March 1st–2nd		Batt. marched from Lilils at BRAY to ASQUITH FLATS (Bde Reserve) Billeted in dugouts. ASQUITH FLATS. Rem Bn left ASQUITH FLATS. Evening of 2nd & took over trenches BOUCHAVESNES NORTH sector. Took over from 2nd DEVONS	Weather fair
	3rd		In trenches. Quiet. Weather fair. One German walked into Casualle Kilted 1 OR. our line - was captured night 3/3. wounded 6 OR	
BOUCHAVESNES TRENCHES	4th		Battalion in conjunction with 2nd No. Hauls & 2/Royal Berks R attacked the German positions E of BOUCHAVESNES. Attack was delivered at 5.30 a.m. under a creeping barrage. Order of Coys: A left Coy, D centre Coy, C right Coy, B support Coy. Attack was quite successful after heavy bombing fights in places. A great many Germans were killed, 2 machine guns were captured after their crews had been killed, together with about 160 prisoners taken by the Battalion: PALLAS TRENCH (German front line) & FRITZ TRENCH (Support line) were captured. From FRITZ TRENCH excellent observation was obtained over country near MOISLAINS &	

WAR DIARY
or
INTELLIGENCE SUMMARY.
(Erase heading not required.)

For Batt. The Worcestershire Regt.
Army Form C. 2118

Place	Date	Hour	Summary of Events and Information	Remarks and references to Appendices
	March		Continued	
			excellent observation for our artillery was obtained. Enemy shelling was very heavy & a heavy barrage was kept up on captured lines & lines of communication all day. The observation obtainable from FRITZ TRENCH enabled the Batt. to beat off counter attacks by means of Lewis guns & rifle fire. Small German parties hurrying up from the direction of MOISLAINS were dispersed by Lewis Gun fire; very few casualties were sustained during the attack. The enemy's heavy shelling was responsible for the larger proportion of our losses. The Batt: was relieved by a Scotch Rifles night 4/5th. A heavy barrage was kept up by the enemy during relief. Bn proceeded to ASQUITH FLATS on relief. Casualties during assault: K. Offs. — W. Offs. 4, OR 44; Mis. OR 158; 11	
ASQUITH FLATS	5th		Billeted in ASQUITH FLATS. Recuperation & cleaning up	
	6th		" "	
	7th		" " Draft 40 O.R joined	

Army Form C. 2118.

1st Bn the Worcestershire Regt

WAR DIARY
or
INTELLIGENCE SUMMARY.
(Erase heading not required.)

Place	Date	Hour	Summary of Events and Information	Remarks and references to Appendices
	1917			
TRENCHES	March 8th		Battalion relieved 2/Devon R. BOUCHAVESNES SECTOR NORTH Evening 8th Weather fair In trenches as above. Weather fair. Casualties K 1 O.R. W 1 O.R.	
	9th		Ditto " " " W 4 O.R.	
	10th		Ditto " Rain " W 1 O.R.	
	11th		Ditto " Draft 1 Off joined " W 1 Off	
	12th		Ditto. Bn relieved night 12/13th by 1/5 Foresters & marched to ASQUITH FLATS	
	13th		Billeted in ASQUITH FLATS. Draft 3 Off + 15 O.R. joined Bn	
	14th		ditto	
	15th		ditto left ASQUITH FLATS 5 p.m. & marched to CAMP 161 (N of CURLU) 4to 6 good in clean condition	
	16th		General clean up	
	17th		Battalion employed building railway near MARICOURT.	
	18th		As above	
	19th		As above	
	20th		As above	

Army Form C. 2118.

WAR DIARY
or
INTELLIGENCE SUMMARY

1st Bn the Worcestershire Regt

(Erase heading not required.)

Instructions regarding War Diaries and Intelligence Summaries are contained in F. S. Regs., Part II. and the Staff Manual respectively. Title pages will be prepared in manuscript.

Place	Date	Hour	Summary of Events and Information	Remarks and references to Appendices
	March			
	21		Continued	
	22		As above	
	23		As above	
	24		As above. 1 Off. joined Battn	
	25		Battn marched from Camp 161 to BOUCHAVESNES. Billeted in cellars & dugouts. Battalion working on roads.	
	26		Batt marched from BOUCHAVESNES to MOISLAINS (evacuated by enemy). Weather fine. Billeted in cellars & in bivouac shelters issued	
	27		Improved billets. 3 offs joined Battn	
	28		Working parties on roads. Very wet. Draft 10f + 146 OR joined	
	29		Working on roads	
	30		ditto	
	31		ditto. Battn in reserve to 23rd + 25th Bgdes. Stood to 4pm - 7pm through night.	
			German aeroplane dropped 8 bombs on MOISLAINS. 4 bombs dropped about 11am 30/31st. No casualties in Battn. No damage to billets. No casualties 31st on MOISLAINS	

C.R.Rafter? for Lt Col
Cmdg 1st Bn The Worc Regt

WAR DIARY or INTELLIGENCE SUMMARY

Army Form C. 2118

1st Battn. 1/Worcestershire Regt.

Vol 29

Place	Date	Hour	Summary of Events and Information	Remarks and references to Appendices
MOISLAINS	1917 April 1st		Battalion marched from billets MOISLAINS to trenches in outpost line between HEUDICOURT & PEIZIERE and advanced 500 yards during night.	K.W
	2nd		Very stormy.	
	3rd		VAUCELETTE FARM scrubbed. Heavy enemy shelling. Casualties K.W. line advanced during night 2/3rd during very heavy rain & snow. Casualties W 3 O.R	
	4th		Battalion relieved night 3/4th by 2nd East Lancashire Regt. marched to billets at LIEREMONT. Billets P. & R.	
	5th		Battalion stood to from 2 a.m. onward during attack by 25th Bgde & 20 Division. Heavy snow all day clearing up. Battalion relieved 2nd East Lancashire Regt	
	6th		Quiet day. Very wet. Bn took over part of line occupied by 2nd No Hants. Patrols went out to BEET FACTORY near VILLERS-GUISLAIN. Slightly more artillery activity. Weather still bad	
	7th	8th		Bad weather. Relieved night of 8/9 by 2nd East Lancashire Regt. Battalion billeted in Nend of HEUDICOURT. Billets P. 3 OR. room W 30 R.	29 W 4 OR

WAR DIARY
or
INTELLIGENCE SUMMARY.

(Erase heading not required.)

Army Form C. 2118.

for B. 7h. Worcestershire Regt

Place	Date	Hour	Summary of Events and Information	Remarks and references to Appendices
HEUDICOURT	9th		Cleaning up equipment clothing. Bn provided carrying parties. Weather changeable.	
	10th		Relieved 2nd East Lancs in trenches night 10/11 on Ridge. Orders	
	11th		Weather bad. Side-slipped to the left & relieved 2nd North'ants night 11/12	
	12th		Fine & Quiet. Patrols went out to GOUZEAUCOURT early morning 12. 2nd East Lancs attacked GOUZEAUCOURT west morning 13 through our line & occupied a line beyond GOUZEAUCOURT	
	13th		Bn relieved by 2nd Nor'ants in support line but billeted in S. end of HEUDICOURT. Billets poor.	
	14th		Cleaning up equipment & clothing. Drill. One or two shells fell in HEUDICOURT. No casualties	
	15th		Bn relieved in HEUDICOURT by 2nd Royal Berks, & marched to NURLU. Billets poor. Bad weather	
	16th		Cleaning up + drill. Weather bad.	

Army Form C. 2118.

1st Bn Worcestershire Regt

WAR DIARY
or
INTELLIGENCE SUMMARY.
(Erase heading not required.)

Instructions regarding War Diaries and Intelligence Summaries are contained in F. S. Regs, Part II. and the Staff Manual respectively. Title pages will be prepared in manuscript.

Place	Date	Hour	Summary of Events and Information	Remarks and references to Appendices
NURLU	April 7th		Bn provided working parties on roads near NURLU	
	9th		Fine but blown up. Occupied by Bns K.5 & 6	
	18th		Bn marched to GUYENCOURT to billets. Billets fair. Weather fair	
	19th		Working parties on mining corps line. Weather fair	
	20th		Bys inspected by G.O.C. Division. Medals presented. Weather good. 2 bombs dropped near village by hostile aeroplane.	
GUYENCOURT	21		Billeted in GUYENCOURT. Billets fair. Weather much improved.	
	22/23		As above.	
	23		Relieved 11th & 2nd Bn Middlesex Regt in the outpost line Head Quarters in VILLERS GUISLAINS. Outpost line Sheet 57c. S.E Squares X11a & b and 17 Central.	
	24/25		In Brigade Outpost Line. Quiet. Village of VILLERS GUISLAINS shelled intermittently daily	
	26		Outpost line pushed on right front (XNC7) forward 100x	
	27		Relieved from outpost line by 2nd Bn E.LANCASHIRE Regt billeted in	

Army Form C. 21

WAR DIARY
or
INTELLIGENCE SUMMARY.
(Erase heading not required.)

Place	Date	Hour	Summary of Events and Information	Remarks and references to Appendices
VILLERS GUISLAINS Billets	27, 28, 29, 30		Good Billeted in VILLERS GUISLAINS. Working all night on the intermediate line of defence known as the BLUE LINE Running round NEST side of village to NEUNIER HOUSE then continuing in an Easterly direction. Also working parties to the outpost line and carrying up R.E. Material to the front line. Map = Sheet No 57 C.S.E.	2 ORs killed 20 ORs wounded

W Cecil Rivers M/A for
Major Connoly 1/15 Own Regt

WAR DIARY
or
INTELLIGENCE SUMMARY.
(Erase heading not required.)

Army Form C. 2118.

HQ 1st Battn
1/5 Not Oxfordshire Regt

Vol 30

Place	Date	Hour	Summary of Events and Information	Remarks and references to Appendices
Trenches between Villers Guislan & Honnecourt	29th		Bn in trenches between VILLERS GUISLAN & HONNECOURT. Very fine weather. Moonlight nights. Large working parties fixing up posts in outpost line serving large salient. Parties were not interfered with by the enemy who were very quiet on our front. Enemy aeroplane very active at Dawn & Dusk occasionally firing at objects on the ground. Saw as a rule in vain by AA.	
	30th		Weather still very good. Very hot. 2 OR wounded. Headquarters in VILLERS GUISLAN Stables occasionally with strafeing etc. Still fine. Large working parties are formed up of	
	31st		Relieved by 2nd Bedfords (199 Bgd 6A) and marched to VAUCELETTE FARM. HQ reserve 2 Coys - 1 HQ at VAUCELETTE FARM 2 Coys in line behind VILLERS GUISLAN (GOUZEAUX July brought up) to front line for work.	
	1st		In Bgde reserve. MW Gun N.H.A. VAUCELETTE FARM	

80 W
at back

Army Form C. 2118.

WAR DIARY
or
INTELLIGENCE SUMMARY.

1st Battn the [?] Regt

(Erase heading not required.)

Place	Date	Hour	Summary of Events and Information	Remarks and references to Appendices
MEAULTE FARM	May 7		at intervals with considerable skill & rapidity	
	8		HQ. very heavy rain at night. B Coy did not relieve the other Battn. here for the day & are awaiting dry weather	
	9		Bttn began wet-running practises again. Weather showery	
	10		Relieved in trenches between R. & Rifle & remained at SOREL LE GRAND. Bttn quite good.	
	11		Fine weather. Range working party went to this BUZZACOURT Railway (dismantled) before good work was done	
			An Inspn. made by GOC 2nd Bde. who did order us to shut helmets	
	12		Relieved in SOREL by 13th Bn. East Surrey Regt marched to MOISLAINS during well fine weather. Billets hew	
	13		Sunday. Church parade morning as rain as 6pm	
	14		Bttle-ing training in fighting in woods etc	
	15		Bttn Benton & Lewis Gunners at training. Carried out in musketry & machine gun

Army Form C. 2118.

WAR DIARY
or
INTELLIGENCE SUMMARY.
(Erase heading not required.)

1st Batt. The Royal Sussex Regt

Place	Date	Hour	Summary of Events and Information	Remarks and references to Appendices
MOISLAINS	May 16		Training as previous day. Scheme	
	17		G.O.C.R.A. & the Gascoynes to one	
			all officers R.S.M's & Sgts on Gatling heavy bomb	
			M.G. when formed up. Coy Commanders "C"	
			Coy attend parade to his instructor	
	18		Training as usual. Coy football v 2/4 Northumb	
			Result 4-0 — 4 heather good Crowd good	
	19		M "VERY LIGHTS" disputed by a Pier Band	
			Gunners Horse Show — weather good	
			training to bull as usual	
	20		My had Katy Brown to tea, Gas training with	
	21		trained. An Practical attack in conjunction with	
	22		Stokes mortars firing live rounds	
	23		Training for intended coming Somme Works	
	24		& bavaria charges lecture by G.O.C ... NE front afternoon	

Army Form C. 2118.

WAR DIARY
or
INTELLIGENCE SUMMARY.

for Bn the Worcestershire Regt.

(Erase heading not required.)

Place	Date	Hour	Summary of Events and Information	Remarks and references to Appendices
MOISLAINS	May 25		Bn training. Trench to trench attack, NCO's co-operating	
	26		Bn training.	
	27		Coy training. Company / Platoon Drill. Sunday Battalion / aquatic sports in swimming pool near MOISLAINS. Weather very fine. Boxing greasy pole + tug of war events.	
	28		Bn short route march. Preparing to move	
	29		Bn marched from MOISLAINS to CAMP 19. Good camp. Plenty of accommodation east of SUZANNE.	
	30		Bn training @ ? rapid loading ec.	
	31		Bn marched from CAMP 19 to CAMP 13 (near BRAY-CORBIE Rd.)	

WAR DIARY or INTELLIGENCE SUMMARY

Army Form C. 2118.

1st Battn. The Worcestershire Regt.

Vol 31

Place	Date	Hour	Summary of Events and Information	Remarks and references to Appendices
CORBIE.	June 1st		Bn Billeted in CORBIE. Billets good.	
	2nd		Detrained at GODEWAERSWELDE at noon and marched to billets in the MERRIS Area ref Map No 27. X 19, 20, 25 + 26 Sn. G. I + 9 reserve. MERRIS Area as above A certain amount of	
	3/10th		training was carried out but training grounds very cramped.	
	11th		Bn marched to the CAESTRE area and billeted in the vicinity of HAZEWINDE Ref. Sheet No 27. P. 29, 30, 35 + 36. Billets good but cramped.	
	12th		Billeted as in the vicinity of HAZEWINDE.	
	13th		Bn Marched to N Camp Ref Sheet No 2 & NW. 9, 23 a & 8. Practically no accommodation and very few bivouacs. Very heavy down pour of rain.	
	14th		Bn marched to YPRES and billeted at the INFANTRY BARRACKS Accommodation very good.	
	15th		Bn relieved 2 Bn Royal Scottish Fusiliers and C Coy relieved 1 Coy Cornwallis Manchester Regt in the HOOGE Sector. Relief complete 2/30 am. Draft of 71 ORs joined Battalion.	2 ORs wounded

81 W
Sheet

WAR DIARY
or
INTELLIGENCE SUMMARY.
(Erase heading not required.)

Army Form C. 2118.

Place	Date	Hour	Summary of Events and Information	Remarks and references to Appendices
	June 16		Bn in trenches HOOGE Sector Very heavy hostile Artillery fire	Casualties Wounded 1 O.R.
	17		As above	Killed 50.Rs. 2 O.Rs.
	18		As above	Wounded 2 O.Rs.
			Bn. relieved by the 2nd Bn Scottish Rifles When relieved Bn. proceeded to VANCOUVER Camp. Ref. Sheet No. 28 N.W. H/4 A.9.3. On the E. Side of the VLAMERTINGHE – OUDERDOM Rd.	
	19/28th		Billeted in VANCOUVER CAMP. The Bn found working Parties as under:– 2 Platoons attached to No.126 & 168 Heavy Siege Battery. S.E. YPRES. One Coy. attached to No.177 Tunnelling Coy. N.W. POPERINGHE One Coy. Supplied Working Parties daily to the Canadian Rly Troops for Building a Rly from BEDFORD H.O. This was made very difficult owing to the ground being under direct observation from the Enemy and it was consequently heavily shelled. Draft of 84 O.Rs joined the Bn on the 24th. Picture Trenches of the Enemy positions in the vicinity of HOOGE & WESTHOEK were viewed. Throughout the time spent in this Camp	Wounded Killed 1. O.R. Wounded 4 O.R.

T2134. Wt. W708—776. 500000. 4/15. Sir J.C. & S.

WAR DIARY
or
INTELLIGENCE SUMMARY.
(Erase heading not required.)

Army Form C. 2118.

Place	Date	Hour	Summary of Events and Information	Remarks and references to Appendices
	June			
VANCOUVER CAMP.	19/2 8		Enemy shelled Cross Roads at Dump at H14B.4.8 Reg. Sheet No.28 N.W. A few shells fell in the vicinity of the camp but did no damage.	
	29		Marched to YPRES at 8.15 p.m. and took over accommodation from 1st SHERWOOD FORESTERS. HQ & 1 Coy at the GATE 2 Coys ESPLANADE. One Coy remains behind at HALIFAX Camp. H14C.3.5. (Sheet No.28 N.W)	
	30		As above, wet weather. Hostile Artillery fire extended to a certain extent.	

A.B. Ratcliffe Col

Army Form C. 2118.

WAR DIARY
or
INTELLIGENCE SUMMARY.
(Erase heading not required.)

24/8
1st Battn. the Worcestershire Regt.
Vol 32

Place	Date	Hour	Summary of Events and Information	Remarks and references to Appendices
YPRES	July 1st 1917		The Battalion remained in the dugouts in YPRES. Bn: HQ. and one Coy at LILLE GATE and two companies at the ESPLANADE. YPRES was very heavily shelled throughout the day. One man was wounded.	
"	July 2nd		Battalion still in YPRES. Shelling not so heavy.	
"	" 3rd		" " " "	
"	" 4th		" " " One man killed and ten wounded by shell fire.	
"	" 5th		The Bn. relieved at 10 P.M. by the 2nd Royal Berkshire Regt. and proceeded to WINNIPEG CAMP via the which is on the OUDERDOM - VLAMERTINGHE road. During this relief heavy shelling took place. One officer (2/Lt "KENT") and eight other ranks were killed and thirty eight wounded, including the R.S.M.	
WINNIPEG CAMP	" 6th		The Bn. remained in WINNIPEG CAMP.	
WINNIPEG CAMP	" 7th		The Bn: moved by bus at 1.15 P.M. to STEENBECQUE. Weather good. Three O/Ranks wounded.	
STEENBECQUE	" 8th		Moved by bus at midday to CUHEM weather dull a little rain	
CUHEM.	" 9th		Billeted in CUHEM. rainy and misty. Draft of 25 O.R. joined Bn.	
"	" 10th		Training bombers, Lewis gunners etc. weather good.	
"	" 11th		" " One officer and two O.R. accidentally wounded while packing bombing "Draft of 5 O.R. joined Bn.	

A.5834 Wt.W4973/M687 750,000 8/16 D.D. & L. Ltd. Forms/C.2118/13

Army Form C. 2118.

WAR DIARY
or
INTELLIGENCE SUMMARY.
(Erase heading not required.)

1st Batn. The Worcestershire Regt.

Place	Date	Hour	Summary of Events and Information	Remarks and references to Appendices
CUHEM	July 12th 1917		Training continued. weather good	
"	13th		" " " "	
"	14th		" " " "	
"	15th		" " Lecture # on Bayonet fighting by Col Campbell. The Bn. marched past the C. in. C.	
"	16th		Training continued. weather good	
"	17th		" " rain	
"	18th		" " Bn: moved to the COYECQUE area, Bn HQ at CAPELLE-SUR-LA-LYS. (Chateau) Draft of 1 Off & 45 O.R. joined Bn	
COYECQUE area.	19th		Training finished. weather good. Draft of 2 O.R.	
"	20th		Bn: moved at 9am by bus to ST. MARTIN and NEUFPRÉ near AIRE. weather good	
ST.MARTIN.	21st		Bn: moved at 2 P.M. by bus to RENINGHELST area, bivouaced in a field. weather good	
RENINGHELST	22nd		Moved at 9 P.M. marched to HALIFAX Camp which is on the OUDERDOM - VLAMERTINGHE road. weather good	

Army Form C. 2118.

WAR DIARY
or
INTELLIGENCE SUMMARY.
(Erase heading not required.)

1st Batt. The Northants Regt

Place	Date	Hour	Summary of Events and Information	Remarks and references to Appendices
HALIFAX CAMP	23rd July 1917		Bn. moved at 10 am. and marched to YPRES. Bn. HQ. at LILLE GATE. Enemy fired many gas shells into YPRES during the night. Weather good.	
YPRES.	24th		Fairly quiet day, more gas shells during the night. Weather good. Casualties 1 killed, 1 wounded.	
"	25th		Fairly quiet day, working parties etc. during night. Weather good. Casualties 4 o.r. wounded.	
"	26th		Bn. moved to HALFWAY HOUSE at 10 A.M.	
HALFWAY HOUSE	27th		Still in dugouts at HALFWAY HOUSE. Weather very good. Casualties 1 killed 5 wounded. Battalion relieved 2nd Bn Northamptonshire Regt in line during evening. Line MENIN Rd — ZOUAVE WOOD.	
	28th		Weather stormy. Enemy artillery active. Trenches badly damaged. Casualties 1 o.r killed 8 wounded	
	29th		Weather good. Still in line. Inter company relief. Casualties 1 or k. 6 or w	
	30th		Weather poor. Battalion formed up at night near KINGSWAY. KINGSWAY SUPPORT for attack. Bn HQ moved from HALFWAY HOUSE DUGOUTS to B.R. CROSS ROADS dugout at 8pm. Order of	

Army Form C. 2118.

WAR DIARY
or
INTELLIGENCE SUMMARY.
(Erase heading not required.)

1st Bn the Worcestershire Regt

Place	Date	Hour	Summary of Events and Information	Remarks and references to Appendices
NEAR HOOGE	July 30th		Coys. Front Pt. C Coy. Left D Coy Support Rt. A Left B C + D Coys to attack & capture IGNORANCE RESERVE + IGNORANCE TRENCH + form a + A + B Coys to pass through to JAMES TRENCH + form a BLUE line on BELLEWAARDE RIDGE	
	31st		Attack commenced at 3.50 am when light was just beginning to show in the east. Batt. attacked the enemy behind a creeping barrage of shrapnel. On the left were the 58th Regt. + on the right the 16th Manchesters. Batt. captured IGNORANCE TRENCH + IGNORANCE SUPPORT without much opposition. An encountered some MG fire + fire from snipers from the right flank + the enemy barrage although at first weak, fell behind IGNORANCE TRENCH causing some casualties. A good many dugouts were found + by the moppers-up, who worked in prescribed	

Army Form C. 2118.

WAR DIARY
or
INTELLIGENCE SUMMARY. 1st Bn Worcestershire Regt
(Erase heading not required.)

Place	Date	Hour	Summary of Events and Information	Remarks and references to Appendices
			Area 1 platoon per coy being "moppers-up". The tunnel under the YPRES-MENIN Rd was expected to give a great deal of trouble but turned out to be quite an easy matter to deal with. 41 prisoners being taken from it. The ground was being traversed by M.G. fire had been very badly cut up by our shell fire & in places was very marshy. After IGNORANCE Support had been taken B & A Coys passed through to attack ST JAMES TRENCH still following the creeping barrage. M.G. fire was still being encountered & the Lewis gun sections succeeded in keeping them under to a great extent. By this time the Coys had got mixed together to a certain extent but this did not prevent the Battn from capturing JAMES TRENCH which was strongly held & JAMES TRENCH was situated on the edge of CHATEAU WOOD, on which the enemy brought a heavy barrage although most of which dropped behind the front attacking	

WAR DIARY or INTELLIGENCE SUMMARY

Army Form C. 2118.

for the 1/4th Worcestershire Regt.

Place	Date	Hour	Summary of Events and Information	Remarks and references to Appendices
HOOGE	July 31		lines. Communication trenches leading from JAMES TRENCH to the top of the BELLE WARDE RIDGE were cleared & Bn commenced to dig in on the forward slope of the ridge overlooking WESTHOEK. A protective barrage was put some 300 yards in front. After a few minutes the 2nd Bn East Lancashire Regt.– based through to attack the BLACK LINE at WESTHOEK. A great deal of MG fire was encountered from the right flank where our troops were not progressing quite up to expectations. Meanwhile A & B coys dug in on the ridge & C & D were consolidating IGNORANCE SUPPORT. When it was certain that troops were well on their way towards WESTHOEK D coy was withdrawn to work as stretcher bearers. The tanks now began to pass through to assist in attacking the GREEN line (after the BLACK) The ground proved too marshy to	

WAR DIARY or INTELLIGENCE SUMMARY

1st Bn The Worcestershire Regt

Place	Date	Hour	Summary of Events and Information	Remarks and references to Appendices
Hooge	July 31		allow of their being used with success & they were heavily shelled on their way up. Bn HQ now moved up from BIR X ROADS encountering a great deal of shell fire on the way up. Bn HQ were first situated in JACOB TRENCH near BODE HQ which had also moved up. During this time the enemy shell fire was fairly heavy & MG's snipers were very active. Bn HQ soon moved to an old German concrete dug out in JABBER DRIVE. C Coy were brought up to assist A & B Coys in consolidation of BLUE LINE. Weather was very cloudy preventing aeroplane work. As the 25th Bgde had not been successful in advancing to the GREEN LINE the Bn formed a right defensive flank in support. During the rest of the day the Bn continued to consolidate the BLUE LINE under heavy shell fire and indirect MG fire. During the evening heavy rain commenced to fall & continued throughout the night. One MG was captured the crew being shot by a Lewis Gunner. Prisoners captured 70 OR Casualties K 3 Off 22 OR W 5 Off 157 OR missing 1 Off 49 OR	

WAR DIARY

INTELLIGENCE SUMMARY.

1st Bn Worcestershire R Army Form C. 2118.
B.E.F.

Place	Date	Hour	Summary of Events and Information	Remarks and references to Appendices
	August 1st		Battalion held Defensive Flank. Conditions very bad indeed. Heavy M.G. & Rifle fire. Rained heavily all day. Relieved in the afternoon by the 3rd Bn Worcestershire Regt and returned to DEVONSHIRE CAMP.	
	2nd		At DEVONSHIRE CAMP. G.O.C. 8th Division visited the Bn.	
	3		Emplaned at 7PM for STEENVOORDE. Billets very good but scattered. Visited by G.O.C. 2nd Corps. 4 Ofrs, 196 ORs joined Battalion.	
	4.		Billeted in STEENVOORDE	
	5.		One Officer joined.	
	6		Reorganisation, training of Specialists. 52 O Ranks joined Bn.	
	7/13		Continued training. 10 Offrs joined Bn on 9th.	
	14.		Marched to HALIFAX CAMP at 7.30 a.m. One working party consisting of two Coys proceeded from STEENVOORDE to YPRES in lorries to make Duck Board Track from RLY WOOD to the WESTHOEK Ridge.	Casualties Killed 1 O.R. Wounded 3 ORs
	15.		Moved to ESPLANADE, YPRES at 9/45 P.M. where the Bn was in Divisional Reserve to the Attack on the following Morning. Found Working Party consisting of two Coys to continue the Duck Board Track were wounded drove	

Army Form C. 2118.

WAR DIARY
or
INTELLIGENCE SUMMARY.
(Erase heading not required.)

(2).

Instructions regarding War Diaries and Intelligence Summaries are contained in F. S. Regs., Part II. and the Staff Manual respectively. Title pages will be prepared in manuscript.

Place	Date	Hour	Summary of Events and Information	Remarks and references to Appendices
	August 16th		Moved up to BIRR CROSS Roads at 12/30 P.M. At 5PM put under orders of G.O.C. 23rd Inf. Bde. at 10PM. moved off Battn. via Rly Wood and occupied a position just under the Crest of WESTHOEK Ridge in the vicinity of J.8.1 Central where the Bn remained in Brigade Support 300 in rear of the 2nd Bn Scottish Rifles who were holding the BLACK LINE. The Hohns being to counter attack the BLACK LINE if the 2nd Bn Scottish Rifles were driven out of this line and to hold it at all costs. No counter offensive developed.	
Ry Sheet Zillebeke	17		Moved into the BLACK LINE and relieved the 2nd Bn Scottish Rifles The line held being along the Road from the Rly Bank exclusive in I.B. D.2.5.D 6.5.05 - J.13 9.5-45. Relief complete soon after Midnight Weather very good. Casualties Killed 13 O.Rs. Wounded 37 O.Rs.	
	18.		Relieved at night by the 17th Bn London Regt. 47 Division. Relief complete at 2am. Returned to CAVALRY BARRACK'S YPRES Casualties Wounded 2 O.Rs.	
Ry Hut No 27	19		At 6PM moved to HALIFAX CAMP	
	20		Moved at 3/30 PM to the CAESTRE AREA Battalion billeted around LA BREARDE P.S.C.7,8. Under Orders of G.O.C. 24th Infantry Bde. Draft of 317 O.Rs joined Bn. from Territorial Reserve Battalions on this date who are a very good draft.	
	21.		The Commander in Chief inspected the Division on parade joined the II Australian Corps. G.O.C 24th Infantry Bde inspected	

[A 5834 Wt. W4973/M687 750,000 8/16 D.D. & L. Ltd. Forms/C.2118/13]

Army Form C. 2118.

WAR DIARY
or
INTELLIGENCE SUMMARY.
(Erase heading not required.)

Instructions regarding War Diaries and Intelligence Summaries are contained in F. S. Regs., Part II. and the Staff Manual respectively. Title pages will be prepared in manuscript.

Place	Date	Hour	Summary of Events and Information	Remarks and references to Appendices
	August 21		The newly joined Draft at 6 pm. 1 Offr joined the Battalion.	
	22		Billeted in CAESTRE, no operations. Draft of 5 ORs joined	
	23		Tng training, Specialists classes. Draft of 10 Offrs & 7 ORs joined	
Rly. Sheet No 28 S30 SE.	24		—	
	25.		Entrained at 3/45 am and moved to Regina Camp T.29.D.9.5, relieving the 2nd AUKLAND Bn.	
	26		Relieved the 18th Bn AUKLAND Regt in the line, S.W. of WARNETON	
			Relief complete at 2/10 a.m.	
	27		In trenches. Situation quiet. Weather very bad. Casualties Killed 1 OR Wounded 2 "	
	28		Weather Rainy & Dull. 7 Officers & 5 ORs joined Battalion.	
	29.		In trenches. Weather stormy. Enemy attitude quiet. 16 ORs joined Casualties Nil.	
	30		— — —	5 ORs wounded
	31		— — better	1 Offr killed 1 OR to hospital

W C Wemuth? Sn Lr Col
Comdg 1/Worc Regt.

A 5834. Wt. W4973/M687 750,000 8/16 D. D. & L. Ltd. Forms/C.2118/13

Army Form C. 2118

WAR DIARY
INTELLIGENCE SUMMARY

Month of SEPTEMBER. 1st Battalion The Worcestershire Regt.

Place	Date	Hour	Summary of Events and Information	Remarks and references to Appendices
Trenches	1, 2, 3.		In trenches WARNETON Sector. Draft of 10 Offrs, 70 Rank & File joined Battalion	Casualties 3 O.Rs W. 10 O.Rs 4 O.Rs K. 5 O.Rs W.
			Relieved at night by 1/4 2nd Bn Northampton R. moved to Bde Support Reserve at ROHARN CAMP.	
	4/8		Bde Reserve at ROHARN CAMP. Battalion in Training and working parties. Weather fine. 1 Officer joined Bn.	
			As above. 10 Officers joined Battalion	
	9/10		Relieved by 2nd Bn Royal Irish Rifles and proceeded to BULFORD LINES situate on the E side of the NEUVE EGLISE – STEENWERCK Rd. Divisional Reserve.	
	11			
	12/17		Bn in camp - BULFORD LINES - Training. 1 Officer & 60 O.Rs joined the Bn.	
	18.		Marched to DE SEULE CAMP situate at Cross Roads of the NEUVE EGLISE – STEENWERCK Road and main BAILLEUL Road. 20 Bn joined.	
	19/23.		At DE SEULE CAMP. Battalion Training. Found small working parties and improved camp. Weather fine.	50 O.Rs joined
	24		Bde Sports. Officers of Bn won the Tug of War	
	25		Bn in training	60 O.Rs joined
	26		General Hunter Weston inspected the camp	2 O.Rs joined

WAR DIARY
or
INTELLIGENCE SUMMARY.
(Erase heading not required.)

Army Form C. 2118

Place	Date	Hour	Summary of Events and Information	Remarks and references to Appendices
	27.		Moved from DE SEULE Camp and subs relieved 2nd Bn Rifle Bde in the trenches – WARNETON SECTOR. Relief complete 11 pm.	1 D.R.
	28.		Situation quiet. Weather good. Work chiefly wiring.	Casualties 10/pm W. 10. K. 1 O.R.
	29.		—	
	30.		Trenches, Ballron (Pylon) shelt over from Enemy. carrying wire copies of the targets des ARDENNES. Wiring continued.	2 O.Rs. K. Wh. C. Sanderford M.C. (temp) 1 hour

WAR DIARY
or
INTELLIGENCE SUMMARY.

1st Bn The Worcestershire Regt. Army Form C. 2118.

WO 160

Place	Date	Hour	Summary of Events and Information	Remarks and references to Appendices
	1-5 October		Battalion in the Trenches WARNETON Sector. The Attitude of the enemy was quiet on the whole. Our defensive amount of Mortar fire by Day from WARNETON & WALART FARM. Machine Gun fire we consider able to wit. Practically two complete Belts of Fire were put out on the Battalion Front & wet Lts Potts ameliorated.	
			Draft 5 ORanks joined 1st inbursh Casualties " 2nd " 1 " " 6 ORs wounded " 3 " " 1 - Gassed " 7 " " 1 - Killed	
	5		Battalion relieved by 2/Northamptonshire R. marched back to Bde Support at RED LODGE	
	5-12 "		Battalion at RED LODGE. Weather fair. Supplied working Parties of two Companies nightly for work on and carrying Material to the Front Line. Improvements were carried out to RED LODGE.	
	12 "		Relieved by 1st Bn. Royal Irish Rifles and marched back to DE SEULE CAMP situate on the Cross Roads of the BAILLEUL, NEUVE EGLISE Roads. Divisional Reserve.	
	13 "		Battalion at DE SEULE CAMP. Working Parties of over 300 ORs found. Draft of 40 ORs joined the Bn.	

Army Form C. 2118.

WAR DIARY
or
INTELLIGENCE SUMMARY.
(Erase heading not required.)

Place	Date	Hour	Summary of Events and Information	Remarks and references to Appendices
	14-29 October		Battalion at DE SEULE CAMP. Training was greatly hampered by the working parties which were found by the Battalion every through 160 O.Rs. Improvements were carried out to the camp and all Officers quarters continued. Classes were formed for Specialists & Bombers Lewis Gunners Rifle Grenadiers. Head quarter Classes were formed for the instruction of Junior NCOs Signallers & Runners. Draft – 1 O.R. joined on 14th. Casualties 9 O.Rs. wounded. 3 Officers " " " 25th	
	28			
	29		M.O.C. 9th Division presented Medal Ribbons. The Bn relieved the 2nd Bn Rifle Bde in the WARNETON SECTOR relief complete at 10.30 p.m. Enemy quiet weather good.	
	30		Draft 1 Officer joined. 1 O Rank wounded.	
	31		In Trenches weather fine Casualties 2 ORs wounded Work continued on wire and posts.	

W. Cruikwin Capt.
for Major 1/S of R

Ref Sheet. PLOEGSTEERT. HAZEBROUCK So.

WAR DIARY or **INTELLIGENCE SUMMARY.**

1st Bn The Worcestershire Regt

Place	Date	Hour	Summary of Events and Information	Remarks and references to Appendices
November	1st		In the trenches WARNETON Sector. Enemy attitude quiet. 1 O.R. gassed.	
	2nd		Relieved at 9/30 PM by the 2nd Bn Northamptonshire R. remained in Bde Support RED LODGE	
	3/5th		Bn at RED LODGE. Found working and carrying parties of 320 ORs daily to work on front line.	
	6th		Relieved 2nd Bn Northamptonshire Regt in the trenches WARNETON Sector. Relief complete 9/30 PM. Situation quiet.	
	7/9th		Bn in Trenches. Weather wet. Enemy attitude quiet. 2 ORs wounded.	
	10th		Relieved by 2nd Bn Northamptonshire Regt and returned to ROMARIN CAMP (Bde Reserve). The 2 Coys in front line came back by train. Weather wet.	
	11/12th		At ROMARIN CAMP. 320 ORs supplied as working and carrying parties to front line.	
	13		Relieved by 40th Australian Bn and marched to DE SEULE Camp	
	14		Bn at DE SEULE CAMP preparations for move. Weather fair.	
	15.		Bn moved at 9/30 am by Route March to the BERQUIN AREA Bn billeted at the CEMETERY (F.12.a.9.7) near NOOTE BOOM.	

35 W 3 sheet

Ref Sheet - No 28 NE 28 NW

1st Bn The Worcestershire Regt — Army Form C. 2118.

WAR DIARY or INTELLIGENCE SUMMARY

Place	Date	Hour	Summary of Events and Information	Remarks and references to Appendices
November	16.		Billeted in the CEMETERY AREA.	
	17.		Marched at 9.30 am to CAESTRE entrained and detrained at YPRES marched to D Camp just to the N. of ST JEAN Camp good weather fine.	
	18.		Bn at D Camp Found working Parties of 250 ORs to Concretion 7.A.	1 OR wounded 1 O.R.
	19.		Moved off to trenches at 2 P.M. and relieved 2nd Bn Worcestershire R. Relief complete at 10 P.M. Sector N. PASSCHENDAELE In trenches Positions to wired on the left about 150 and on the Right 300yds. Shellfire very heavy. Two Patrols of 20 & 5th Regt 444th Div Captured.	Killed 1 OR 3 ORs Wounded 13 ORs 2 Offrs
	21.		In trenches Supports had to be moved forward as were to the front line as positions owning to very heavy Barrage fire	Killed 6 ORs Wounded 25 ORs 26 ORs Casualties
	22.		Relieved by 1/Sherwood Foresters at 9/30 PM. and returned to Bde Support at BELLE VUE Bn accommodated in Pill Boxes & shellholes.	Killed 1 OR 12 ORs Wounded 31 ORs 17 ORs
	23.		Relieved at 9 PM by 2nd B.W. Worcestershire Regt marched back to E Camp adjoining D Camp at ST JEAN.	Missing 5 ORs

Army Form C. 2118

WAR DIARY
or
INTELLIGENCE SUMMARY.
(Erase heading not required.)

Instructions regarding War Diaries and Intelligence Summaries are contained in F. S. Regs., Part II. and the Staff Manual respectively. Title pages will be prepared in manuscript.

Place	Date	Hour	Summary of Events and Information	Remarks and references to Appendices
	24/2/18		Battalion at E Camp found working Parties of 300 ORs daily to front line. 2 OPs joined 2 ORs wounded.	
	29th		Bn found working parties of 300 ORs and 10 ORs joined.	
			Bn entrained at BRANDHOEK and moved to BRANDHOEK Casualties 10 Rs wounded	
	30		Bn entrained at BRANDHOEK and detrained at WIZERNES. Marched to LONGUENESSE and billeted there.	
	31/12/17			

W Cleeves Capt
M Aep/Worc R

A 5834 Wt. W4973/M687 750,000 8/16 D. D. & L. Ltd. Forms/C.2118/13

Army Form C. 2118.

WAR DIARY
or
INTELLIGENCE SUMMARY.
(Erase heading not required.)

1st Bn the Worcestershire Regt.

Vol 31

Place	Date	Hour	Summary of Events and Information	Remarks and references to Appendices
LONGUENESSE	Dec 1st		Battalion billeted in Longuenesse. weather fair. Cleaning up & issuing new clothing 1 Officer joined Bn	
	2nd		weather fair	
	3rd		Battalion commenced training musketry Coy Drill etc	
	4th		Do above	
	5th		Do above	
	6th		Do above	
	7th		Do above	
	8th		Divine Service 1 Officer joined Bn	
	9th		Bn in training Platoon in attack 4 Off joined Bn	
	10th		Do above Comdg officers inspection full marching Order	
	11th		Do above Bn inspected by G.O.C. 24th Infantry Brigade	
	12th		Do above Bn Carried out field firing practice on the range Each coy. carried out an imaginary	
	13th		Do above attack. independently according to instructions in Company in the attack	
	14th		Do above Bn in training weather colder 1 Officer joined Bn	
	15th		Do above	

WAR DIARY
or
INTELLIGENCE SUMMARY.

Army Form C. 2118

Place	Date	Hour	Summary of Events and Information	Remarks and references to Appendices
LONGUENESSE	Dec 16th 1917		Battalion billeted in Longuenesse. Constitutional weather four Divine Services	
	17th		As above. Bn in training. SOR's joined Bn	
	18th		As above. Slight snow. Weather cold. Frosty. Bn in training. 10R joined	
	19th		As above. Weather cold. Bn in training.	
	20th		As above. Bn in training. Imaginary attack by Bn. Objectives 4 lines of enemy trenches. 10R joined Bn	
	21st		As above. Bn in training.	
	22nd		As above. Brigade Section Rifle Shooting Competition & Officers Revolver Competition. 2 Section under 5 men. All were 1st & Lt. Skelding was the best individual scorer.	
	23rd		Bn Burial Services. Bn Xmas Dinners in billets.	
	24th		Day of cleaning up & preparation for move. Transport moved	
	25th		Bn marched to WIZERNES and entrained for ST JEAN at 6am. Visited at station by Corps Commander. Bn detrained at ST JEAN and marched to billets HQ & 2 Coys in dugouts at CAPRICORN (SPREE FARM) 2 Coys in camp at CALIFORNIA. Fair & cool day. Heavy fall of snow	

Army Form C. 2118.

WAR DIARY
or
INTELLIGENCE SUMMARY.
(Erase heading not required.)

1st Bn. The Worcestershire Regt

Place	Date	Hour	Summary of Events and Information	Remarks and references to Appendices
PASSCHEN-DAELE	Dec 1917 26		Bn relieved 7th Bn R.B. in the right sector of the Divisional front owing to very bright moonlight on snow the relief was spotted in spite of a very heavy barrage the relief was carried out being completed by 10.30 p.m. Casualties 6 killed & missing 28 wounded	
	27		Quieter day. Very hard frost. Casualties W 1 W Off. 2 O.R. K. 1 Off. W.O.R. 10 O.R.	
	28		Fairly quiet. Still hard frost. More snow	
	29		Gas shelling of trenches. More snow	
	30		Slight thaw. Bn relieved by 2nd Lincolnshire Regt. Every guard during relief. Bn entrained at WIELTJE and detrained at BRANDHOEK & marched to billets at BRAKE CAMP (VLAMERTINGHE WOOD) B. Hut fairly good	
	31		Hard frost. Bn concert. New Year concert held. treatment of feet & cleaning up carried on	

Observed
Capt. & Adjt.
Worcestershire Regt

A 5834 Wt. W4973/M687 750,000 8/16 D. D. & L. Ltd. Forms/C.2118/13.

To
M/4
D.A.G.
3rd Echelon
Base

Herewith War Diary for month
of JANUARY 1918.

W.C.Stevens
Captain for Capt
Comdg 1st Bn The Worcestershire Regt.

1/2/1918.

Army Form C. 2118

1st Batt Worcestershire Regt

Vol 38

WAR DIARY
or
INTELLIGENCE SUMMARY.
(Erase heading not required.)

Place	Date	Hour	Summary of Events and Information	Remarks and references to Appendices
	Jan 1st - 3rd		Batt. billeted in BRAKE CAMP ref Sheet No 28 N.W. A30 d.7.5. Training. Hostile aircraft dropped bombs on edge of Camp. Casualties 2 OR wounded	
	4th		Batt. moved to JUNCTION CAMP ref Sheet No 28 N.W. C27 c.1.2. Working Party. Found 1 OR wounded.	
	5th - 6th		Batt. at JUNCTION CAMP Working Parties. 1 OR wounded.	
	7th		Batt. moved into line and relieved the 2nd Batt. W. YORKS. REGT in the PASSCHENDAELE sector. 3 OR joined Batt.	
	8th - 10th		Batt. in trenches. Attitude of enemy quiet. Heavy shots fell. 11 OR wounded.	
	11th		Relieved by 2nd Battn MIDDLESEX REGT. 2 OR joined at BRANDHOEK and moved to DRAKE CAMP. Entrained at WIELTJE Station (detrained)	
	12th - 14th		Batt. billeted in BRAKE CAMP. 3 OR wounded. Weather ord. 4 OR joined	
	15th		Batt. moved to CALIFORNIA CAMP Ref Shel No 28 N.W. C23 c.2.4. 2 OR fell. 7 officers and 1 OR joined.	
	16th		Batt. in CALIFORNIA CAMP. Found working parties. Weather wet and cold. Batt.	
	17th		Moved to ST JEAN STATION & billeted in POPERINGHE. Entrained for POPERINGHE at 4.30 am 1 Officer joined	

WAR DIARY
INTELLIGENCE SUMMARY

Army Form C. 211

Place	Date	Hour	Summary of Events and Information	Remarks and references to Appendices
	16th - 24th		Battn. billeted in POPERINGHE. Finds working parties of three Coys. per diem. 2 Officers & 16 O.R. joined.	
	25th		Battn. found working parties. 1 Officer joined.	
	26th		Battn. entrained and detrained at GODDESVERVELDE marched to EECKE and billeted N.W. of the village. H.Q. in EECKE.	
	27th - 30th		General refitting, reorganising, and re-clothing the Battn. 1 Officer & 50 OR joined.	
	31st		Inspection by the G.O.C 24th BRIGADE.	

W. Clavere Capt A/Major
1/Worc Regt

WAR DIARY
or
INTELLIGENCE SUMMARY.
(Erase heading not required.)

1st BATTN. THE WORCESTERSHIRE REGT.

Army Form C.2118

Place	Date	Hour	Summary of Events and Information	Remarks and references to Appendices
	Feb 1st		Battalion billeted at EECKE. Two boys engaged on shell hole consolidation. Two boys practising an attack on a strong point. Draft of 25 o.r. joined.	
	2nd		Two boys engaged on shell hole consolidation in morning, and two officers.	
	3rd		General preparation and cleaning up for inspection by that G.O.C. 8th Division.	
	4th		G.O.C. 8th Division's inspection	
	5th		Ranks allotted to Battalion.	
	6th		Battalion special training in Bombers, Lewis Gunners, Signallers, Observers & Scouts leave.	
	7th		the boy firing on range, the remainder of Battalion — Two boys plus the Consolidation, one boy attack on strong point.	
	8th		General preparation for move on the 9th inst. Draft of 4 o.r. joined.	
	9th		Battalion move from EECKE at 7.30 am. entrained at GOODSVERWELDE detrained at WIELTJE and accommodated at ENGLISH FARM CAMP. Transport lines situate at RYDE CAMP.	
	10th		Battalion moved off at 4.30 pm relieving the BORDER REGT in the WESTROOSEBEKE Sector. left Bde of 8th Corps front.	

Army Form C. 2118

WAR DIARY
or
INTELLIGENCE SUMMARY.
(Erase heading not required.)

1st BATTN.
THE WORCESTERSHIRE REGT.

Instructions regarding War Diaries and Intelligence Summaries are contained in F. S. Regs., Part II. and the Staff Manual respectively. Title pages will be prepared in manuscript.

Place	Date	Hour	Summary of Events and Information	Remarks and references to Appendices
	11th		Battalion in trenches. Attitude of enemy quiet. Inter company reliefs. Weather good.	
	12th			
	13th		At 6 A.M. the enemy raised MOR 12 & 13 posts having been so sharp. The front line was only occupied by day light and was thought out overnight by 2/Lt S.G. RUSSELL. B Coy. Casualties 1 OR killed, 3 OR wounded, 3 OR missing. 1 Officer and 1 OR joined Battn.	
	14th		Battalion relieved at night by the 14 Battn THE SHERWOOD FORESTERS. and returned to Brigade Support at CALIFORNIA CAMP.	
	15th-21st		Battalion in CALIFORNIA CAMP. Three boys supplied daily for work on the Divi reserve line. Six boys work daily. The remaining Coy and H.Q. employed on cleaning the camp and collection of salvage. Casualties 3 O.R wounded in camp by shell fire.	
	22nd		Battalion relieved 2/Battn NORTHANTS REGT in the WESTROOSEBEKE. Draft of 54 OR joined on 18th inst.	

A 5834. Wt W4973/M687 750,000 8/16 D. D. & L. Ltd. Forms/C.2118/13.

WAR DIARY or INTELLIGENCE SUMMARY

1st BATTN. THE WORCESTERSHIRE REGT.

Army Form C. 2118

Place	Date	Hour	Summary of Events and Information	Remarks and references to Appendices
Sector	22nd		Attitude of enemy Quiet.	
	23rd		In trenches. Reconnoitering Patrol had opposition approximately opposite No 6 post.	
	24th		Inter-Coy reliefs.	
	25th		Hostile party attempted to raid on the Right Front Coy. This party was effectually dealt with by Lewis Gun and Rifle fire. The whole of the left Coy front was wired with the exception of a small gap, double apron fence pattern. Posts and supports and linked up. 2nd Support Coy at WALLAMOLEN. 1 Officer and 6 O.R. wounded. The Reserve Coy at KRON PRINZ FARM, was used for work under R.E. Supervision on the WALLAMOLEN defences. Ration and R.E. carrying parties. Draft of 52 O.R. joined.	
	26th		Relieved by 1st BATTN THE SHERWOOD FORESTERS. Relief completed by 8.5 p.m. Enemy attitude quiet. 2/c Battalion returned to Brigade Reserve at JUNCTION CAMP.	

Army Form C. 21

WAR DIARY
or
INTELLIGENCE SUMMARY.
(Erase heading not required.)

1st BATTN.
THE WORCESTERSHIRE REGT.

Place	Date	Hour	Summary of Events and Information	Remarks and references to Appendices
	27th		Day devoted to Baths, general inspections, clearing up camp and re-organisation.	
	28th		These Coys engaged on the construction of Keeps in the Army Zone. One Coy and H.Q. clearing camp and collection of salvage	

W.Chevens Capt. t/a Capt.
Comdg. 1/Worc.

28/2/18

24th Inf.Bde.
8th Div.

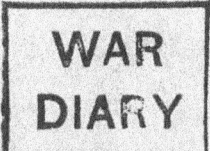

1st BATTN. THE WORCESTERSHIRE REGIMENT.

M A R C H

1 9 1 8

WAR DIARY or INTELLIGENCE SUMMARY.

1st BN: THE WORC: REGT

Ref Sheet AMIENS.

Army Form C. 2118

Place	Date	Hour	Summary of Events and Information	Remarks and references to Appendices
	March 1918 1st-4th		Battalion billeted in JUNCTION CAMP. Working parties found daily for RUPPRECHT KEEP and GREY RUIN	
	5th-12th		Battalion entrained at WIELTJE, detrained ABEELE, and marched to WATOU where a programme of training was carried out as laid down and the 13th inst. Boxing contests were held during this period.	
	13th		Battalion marched to ABEELE and entrained there for LUMBRES. After detraining the Battalion marched to MORINGHEM in G.H.Q. reserve.	
	- 21st		Training was carried out as laid down in programme. Boxing contests were held and cross-country runs were organised during this period.	
	22nd		Battalion proceeded by march route from MORINGHEM to ST OMER where it entrained for NESLE.	

WAR DIARY
or
INTELLIGENCE SUMMARY.

(Erase heading not required.)

Army Form C. 2118.

Place	Date	Hour	Summary of Events and Information	Remarks and references to Appendices
	23.		Bn detrained at NESLE at 2/30 a.m. marched to EPENANCOURT Position was to keep up by Bn along line to form Bank of Canal the Right of Bn resting on PARGNY. In the afternoon A&B Coys took up position E of FALVY were forced in consequence of an action to extricate another Division 7 R.W.F. and Bn extended and former positions on line at no required. The Enemy at about 9.40 P.M entered EPENANCOURT but was ejected by a counter attack lead by 2 Lieut J.C. Roberts.	
	24		The Right Flank of the Batt on Right was forced back and in line the Bn was forced back to LICOURT where a position was held E of that village.	
	25.		After very severe fighting the Bn was forced to retire and took up position on the Rly Line S. of MARCHE LE POT which was held. Before Midnight the Bn was ordered to retire on to Works E of ABLAINCOURT.	
	26.		The Enemy came on again soon after daylight and invested the Works at ABLAINCOURT the Right Flank having given the Bn retired VIA LIHONS (The Enemy was then in possession of CHAULNES) to ROSIÈRES where a position was taken up S.E of that village between FRISY and the Road Junction S.E of ROSIÈRES. The enemy invested this position in the afternoon.	
	27.		The Enemy attacked at 6.30 a.m. and the line was very hard pressed but a counter attack from the right enabled us to retake a few posts occupied by the Enemy. This line was held throughout the day after very severe fighting.	

Army Form C. 2118

WAR DIARY
or
INTELLIGENCE SUMMARY.
(Erase heading not required.)

Instructions regarding War Diaries and Intelligence Summaries are contained in F. S. Regs., Part II. and the Staff Manual respectively. Title pages will be prepared in manuscript.

Place	Date	Hour	Summary of Events and Information	Remarks and references to Appendices
	28.		After severe fighting the Bn retired and took up a position on the high ground N.W. of VRELY. The enemy having entered VRELY the Bn subsequently retired onto a position on the high ground S.E. of CAIX. The Bn was then ordered to evacuate this line and proceeded to HUREUIL then to ROUVREL where it was billeted for the night.	
	29.		The Bn proceeded to JUMEL and billeted there.	
	30.		At 6 am the Bn moved forward via REMIENCOURT to the BOIS DE SENECHAL where it remained till 6.30 PM when it moved forward through CASTEL and relieved the 16th Lancers & 9th Hussars in reserve on the Ravine N. of MOREUIL	
	31.		The Bde on left was shelled out of their positions E. of MOREUIL wood 2 Coys of the Bn formed defensive flank along the W. edge of wood and held it.	
			Total casualties for the period from the 23rd March up to date. Officers Killed 2 Wounded 18 O Ranks Killed nil Wounded 174 Missing 200.	

W.C. Flowers Capt
A/M.C. 16th Lancer R.

Training Programme 24 F B4
All units

1st Battalion The Worcestershire Regiment.

Training Programme for the period Monday 18th to Saturday 23rd March, 1918.

Date.	9 a.m. – 10 a.m.	10.15 a.m. – 11.15 a.m.	11.30 a.m. – 12.45 p.m.	2 – 3 p.m.
18th.	Whole	day	on "Y"	Range.
19th.	20 minutes B.F. Coy Drill Order Parades with steady drill.	Coy. Route Marches. March discipline & extension from column in artillery formation and vice versa. Diamond formations advancing across country with flank & advance guards. Dress Marching Order.	Musketry. Muscle exercises, rapid loading & firing with and without Box Respirators. Miniature Range as allotted.	Specialist training in L.G's and Rifle Grenade. Lecture in general subjects by C.O. to whole Battn.
20th.	Coy. 20 minutes route march, skirmishing and open order drill. Advancing and withdrawing by alternate rushes of Sections. Use of covering fire. Dress Marching order.	Musketry, Muscle Exercises. Rapid loading and firing with and without Box Respirators. Miniature Range as allotted.	Battn Demonstration Platoon in 1. Range discipline & Rapid Fire. 2. March Discipline. 3. Steady Drill and Scouting, whole Bn to attend. Dress, Drill Order.	Specialist Training in Bombing.
21st.	Coys in the attack and capture of Strong Points. Dress, Marching Order.	Battn Demonstration Platoon in Scouting and capture of Strong Point. Musketry. Rapid Firing & loading. Dress, Drill Order.	Lecture by C.O. to whole Battn on night operations and issue of Field Operation Orders to Coys.	Specialist Training in L.G's & R. Grenade. Night operations from 7 p.m. Dress Battle Order.
22nd.	20 minutes B.F. Scouting and Patrolling under Coy. arrangements.	Battalion in the attack. Dress, Full Marching Order. The last ½ hour allotted to musketry.		Specialist training in Bombing.
23rd.	20 minutes B.F. Coy. route marches, march discipline. Extension into artillery formation from column of route. Flank and advance guards.	Platoon competition in the attack on Strong Point. Each Coy to detail one platoon. Dress for competition full marching order. Dress for Bn - Drill Order.	½ an hour musketry, muscle exercises, rapid loading & firing. ½ an hours lecture by C.O. to Bn on general subjects and remarks on training.	Specialist training in L.G. & R. Grenade. Night operations from 7 p.m. Dress, Battle Order.

1. Reveille daily at 6.45 a.m. Breakfast 7.45 a.m. Dinners 1 p.m. Battn Ord: Room 3.15 p.m. Lights Out: 9.10 p.m. Sunday will be a day of rest.

2. On days allotted for Specialist Training, the following Officers, N.C.O's and men will attend a Battn H.Q. Class under the Battn Specialist N.C.O's, all other ranks being trained under Coy. arrangements in the specialist subjects laid down for the day:
   For Lewis Gun. Each Coy 1 Officer and all Lewis Gun Sections and 50% of remaining Sections.
   For Rifle Grenade. Each Coy 1 Officer and 50% of all Sections except Lewis Gun Section.
   For Mills Grenade. Each Coy 1 Officer and 50% of all Sections except Lewis Gun Section.
   N.B. Lewis Gun Sections will train in the Lewis Gun in all Specialist Parades.

3. Battalion H.Q., less a small percentage to be detailed daily by the Adjutant will conform to the above programmes of work and will train under O.C. H.Qrs.
   The Signalling Officer will be responsible for the tactical training of all Battalion Signallers, starting on the fourth day of training.

4. Half of each day Coy. servants and sanitary men and other employed will attend all parades daily except the first. Coy. Cooks will carry out at least 10 minutes rapid loading and firing dayly under Coy arrangements. The transport officer and Quartermaster will arrange daily to train all personnel attached to them in at least 10 minutes rapid loading and firing.
   All grooms will attend 2 days training weekly under Coy arrangements.

5. Drummers will carry out 10 minutes rapid loading and firing under Sgt. Drummer.
   A detailed programme of work will be submitted by 6 p.m. every Wednesday night/for the ensuing week by Coy & Platoon Commdrs to BN H.Q. they will be worked out in detail vide the Battalion programme of work which will be issued every Tuesday.
   It is impressed on all Officers and N.C.O's that before going on any parade whatever, they are to have a cut and dried scheme, either on paper, or in their heads, as to what they intend to do.

6. Subaltern Officers saluting, and all Officers in the Compass and Horse Riding.

7. The above Programme is subject to alteration, but will be adhered to unless otherwise ordered.

ACTION OF THE 1/WORCESTERSHIRE REGT.

NIGHT 23rd/24th MARCH 1918.

The enclosed is a letter and sketch map by Major F.C. Roberts (now R. Warwickshire, formerly Worcestershire Regt), following on conversations between us in the course of the compilation of our Regimental History.

In the previous conversations Major Roberts was very definite as to the following facts:-

1. The counter-attack (for which he was awarded the V.C.) was <u>not</u> at Epenancourt but at Pargny.

2. The 2/Rifle Brigade (referred to in the letter as "the Battn. on our right") only occupied Pargny with a small patrol at dusk 23rd and apparently evacuated it before the German occupation that evening.

3. That all the Diaries of units concerned were written up hastily several days afterwards. (He himself was wounded on the 27th and did not see the battalion diary of 1/Worcester Regt.)

4. That 8th Div. H.Q. were not in effective control until the 25th/26th, and had no accurate knowledge of what happened on the 23rd/24th. On those two days, he said, the battalions of 24th Bde. acted under orders of battalion commanders, in concert as best they could.

After digesting this letter I proceeded to France and went over the ground. The plan enclosed closely resembled Pargny village but is not in the least like Epenancourt.

H. FitzM. STACKE.

Captain.

The Worcestershire Regiment.

<u>10.8.28.</u>

H.Q. 2nd Rhine Brigade,
British Army of the Rhine.
24. 5. 25.

Dear Stacke,

I enclose a plan of PARGNY Village more or less to scale, with certain notes to give you the idea of the counter-attack.

Unfortunately you did not send me what you have already written on the show, so I think I'll run through it rapidly, as I remember it.

After the two companies had returned from Falvy village about 5 p.m. on the 23rd March, where they had been covering the retreat of the 50th Division, I reinforced the battalion front on the W. of the Canal which we held from N. of Epenancourt to Pargny Bridge inclusive. About 6 p.m. I found a few men of another battalion in the southern part of the village and was told the whole battalion was at that time getting into position along the canal to my right. After having fixed up the defence of the Bridge (partially blown up) I walked along the canal bank looking at my posts until I reached my battalion H.Q. in a sunken road just south of Epenancourt, here I had tea, and at dusk started off to go round the battalion again, from N. to S. At about 8 p.m. I reached a point about "E" (on map) and found the post there very excited as they were being shot at from houses in the N. portion of Pargny, and had also seen boche in the village before dark. I was also told that all posts between them and the bridge had ceased to function (afterwards I found a number of men in them had been shot in the back and that the local defence South of the bridge had been broken through about dusk).

I at once realized that the battalion supposed to have been on my right could not have arrived, and that unless the village was taken back, we should be mopped up during the night, if the enemy continued to advance N.W. west of the canal. After about ¼ of an hour I managed to collect about 45 O.R's from posts N. of "E" and at once moved across country to "A" (on map) along "F" (a sunken road) which prevented the party from being seen by the bosche. Here I organized my three parties behind a few broken-down cottages, telling the R. and Left parties to work along the routes given them, paying attention to any noise that might start in the main street (i.e. D party's route) and to keep up level with me, so as to deal with any enemy who might clear out of the houses in the outskirts of the village and try to get away.

As far as I can recollect we actually started off at about 9 p.m. "D" party started off with fixed bayonets and magazines loaded. For the first 100 yards or so we went in two parties in single file on each side of the main road at the walk and as quietly as possible. The first intimation that I had of the Bosche was some shouting from houses we were passing, and then both m.g. and rifle fire (very wild) from windows and doors, with small parties of the enemy dashing into the streets and clearing off in the direction of the Bridge. Once this started we all went hell for leather up the street firing at anything we saw and using the bayonet in many cases, From beginning to end every man screamed and cheered as hard as he bloody well could and by the time we reached the Church the village was in an uproar and bosche legging it hard to the bridge or else chucking his hands up (we only took very few prisoners as I'd told the men to KILL so as to prevent the brutes again coming up in our rear). In the Churchyard itself the hardest fighting took place tombstones being used as if in a game of hide and seek. Here after clearing it we had a few minutes rest and then went smack through to the bridge where a mass of Bosche were trying to scramble across, some did and some didn't ! This more or less ended it, and we at once brought up some of the Reserve Coy. to take over this part of the front. The two flank parties did extremely well as regards turning the bosche into us, and helped to make a success of the general muddle which as a matter of fact went far to help us in getting the village back. We actually captured 6 light machine guns, and about 15-20 prisoners and I think killed approx. 80 -100. Our own losses were heavy but I can't quite remember the exact figures.

I hope this will give you the picture more or less. The village itself and the church was in a more or less state of ruin owing to the fighting during the early part of the war.

Am afraid I'm not sufficiently skilled to make up much of a picture for you but have attempted a rough panorama sketch.

As regards the rest of your diary I've read it through with much interest and think it more or less true to facts. Let me know if I can help you further.

Yours ever,

"Cully"

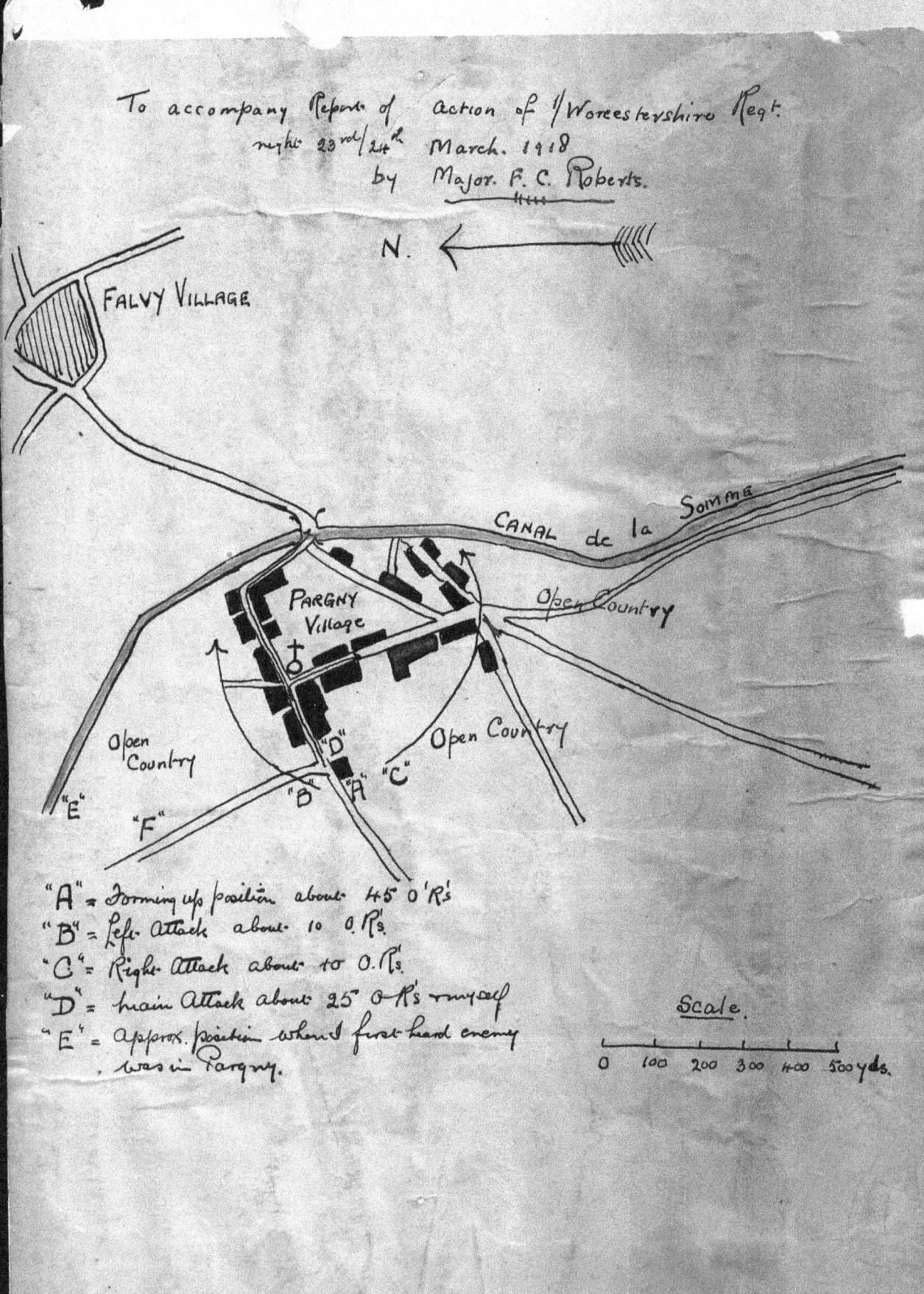

To accompany Report of action of 1/Worcestershire Regt.
night 23rd/24th March. 1918
by Major. F. C. Roberts.

"A" = Forming up position about 45 O.R's
"B" = Left Attack about 10 O.R's
"C" = Right Attack about 10 O.R's
"D" = Main Attack about 25 O.R's & myself
"E" = Approx. position when I first heard enemy was in Pargny.

24th Brigade.

8th Division.
++++++++++++-

1st BATTALION

WORCESTERSHIRE REGIMENT

APRIL 1918.

D.A.G
3rd Echelon
    Base

                    Herewith War Diary for
Month of APRIL 1918.

                        W C Stevens Capt
                              LIEUT. COL.
5/5/1918.   COMDG. 1ST BN. THE WORCESTERSHIRE REGT.

WAR DIARY
or
INTELLIGENCE SUMMARY.
(Erase heading not required.)

Army Form C. 2118.

1/Worcestershire Regt.

Place	Date	Hour	Summary of Events and Information	Remarks and references to Appendices
April	1.		Bn holding a line for the W. Edge of HORGNY Wood. A very quiet day on the whole. The Cavalry made an attack N. of the wood assisted by very numerous aeroplanes, which was successful.	
	2.		Relieved by the French at 3 a.m. – 133rd Regt Chasseurs à pied marched back via CASTEL to DOMMARY in billet moved on about midday to SAINS EN AMIENOIS where we entrained and went via AMIENS to HANGEST Billets good. Billeted in HANGEST – E. Ville Rest.	
	3.		–do–	
	4.		–do–	
	5.			10 Offrs joined Bn. 1740 O.Rs joined Bn.
	6.		M.O.C inspected Draft of 1740 O.Rs. The Bn moved to SOUES after the inspection. Billets found.	10 Hrs joined.
	7/8.		Billeted in SOUES. General cleaning up and Reorganisation. 4 Offrs joined Bn.	
	9.		G.O.C. 8th Division inspected the Bn on Bn Parade	
	10/11.		Billeted in SOUES. The general training for this period was mainly celebration of Divis fire and musketry acquaintance with Artillery Formation.	
	12.		Marched to HANGEST entrained and detrained at ST ROCH and marched to QUERRIEU where the Bn was billeted. Be YTCD and the B89 rejoined Bn from the woods hour of duty in Infants.	40 W/ 3 these

WAR DIARY
or
INTELLIGENCE SUMMARY

Army Form C. 2118.

Place	Date	Hour	Summary of Events and Information	Remarks and references to Appendices
April	13/17		Battalion billeted in QUERRIEU. Training continued. A draft of 140 O.Rs from the MANCHESTER Regt joined the Bn on 17th.	
	18.		Bn moved at 5pm to GLISY, and billeted there.	
	19.		Moved after Bde took up a position in BOIS de BLANGY - Corps Reserve. At 6pm W.G Bde took over the line in front of VILLERS BRETONNEUX. The Bn remained counter attack Bn just S. of VILLERS BRETONNEUX (A & B Coy in position S. of VILLERS BRETONNEUX C & D Coys in CACHY Switch). Batteries went back to CAHON.	
	20/22		Bn remained in wire positions. Casualties 10 R killed, 5 wounded	
	23.		Bn rejoined in wire positions. Casualties 10 R killed, 5 wounded. The Bde was relieved by 23rd Bde. The Bn less C&D Coys relieved by 2/Devon Regt who remained under orders of 23rd Bde to take civil portions. Bois de l'Abbé reserve in Bois de l'Abbé. Casualties S.O.R wounded. Remainder of Bn moved back to Div. Reserve in CACHY.	
	24/25		As above. Casualties 5 ORs wounded. 90 ORs killed. 8 Offrs joined Bn.	
	26.		Bn relieved 14/52 Australian Bde and moved back to Corps Reserve in Bois de BLANGY. 24hrs killed 3 ORs killed 10th joined Bn. 10 ORs wounded	
	27.		Bn moved back to billets in CAHON	
	28/30		Bn billeted in CAHON. Time devoted to Reorganization & general cleaning up. Billets good. 1 OR wounded	

W. Chevin Capt /poor R

D.A.G
3rd Echelon
Base

Herewith War Diary for month of
MAY 1918.

W C Stevens

11-6-18

Captain
Comdg 1st Bn The Worcestershire Regt

WAR DIARY or INTELLIGENCE SUMMARY

1st Bn The Worcestershire Regt   Army Form C. 2118.

By Major BOISSONS

Place	Date	Hour	Summary of Events and Information	Remarks
May	1st		The Bn billeted in CAMON, resting. Weather good.	
	2.		Moved by March Route to GUIGNEMICOURT	
	3.		Moved off from GUIGNEMICOURT and entrained at SALEUX at 10 P.M.	
	4.		Detrained at AISMES at 3 PM and marched to CHERY CHARTREUVE where Bn was encamped in Camp C.	20/Br + 23 OR joined the Bn.
	5.		In camp at CHERY CHARTREUVE. General training commenced.	10R joined Bn
	6.		Bn inspected by G.O.C. XXIInd Inf Bde.	
	7.		Training continued.	
	8.			1 Offr joined Bn
			In the morning area was inspected by the Lt GENERAL DESPARÉZ commanding the VI French Army.	
			Afternoon by Lt GENERAL DESPARÉZ commanding the VI French Army.	
	9.		Moved by March Route and billeted in COURLANDON	
	10.		Moved to ROUCY. Forward Party reconnoitred via JOUVINCOURT Sector	
	11.		Bn moved into line and relieved the 221st French Regiment	
			Relief complete by 2 a.m.	
	12/16		Bn holding JOUVINCOURT. Attitude of enemy very quiet indeed	2 OR wounded
	17		Relieved by 2 Bn Northamptonshire Regt. Bn returned to Dubrissevre	6 OR wounded
			at VENTELAY dash Bn arrived in camp at 6.30 am in morning of 17th instant	

WAR DIARY or INTELLIGENCE SUMMARY

Army Form C. 2118.

Worcestershire R

Place	Date	Hour	Summary of Events and Information	Remarks and references to Appendices
	18/23		Bn in Camp at VENTELAY General Training carried out.	1/9/5/18 1st Reinf. 27/5/18 12 ORs
	24.		Moved to Bde Support and relieved 1/Herewood Fores./ R. 10/hr. joined 2 Coys sent to BERRY AU BAC when orders of 15th Inf Bde. tactical Reserve 2 Coys Relieved by 25th Bde. Bn in div. attitude of Sweeny very quiet.	
	25/24 27		Enemy's Barrage opened at 1 a.m. and as far as can be ascertained attacked at 4 a.m. At 11 a.m. Col Davidge took up a line between ROUSSY + BOUFIGNEREUX with leaving Remnants of 24 + 25th Infantry Bde and all stragglers of the Battalion. This line was forced to retire and successive line was taken up East of the ground N. of MONTIGNY.	
	28.		The left flank was forced back and the line was withdrawn at about 9/20 a.m. to JONCHERY. This line was held till late afternoon when a further withdrawal to the N. of BRANSCOURT was made subsequently a line was held on high ground South of that village but owing to the left flank being forced back a further withdrawal to the reverse slope of the Hill was made here the Trench atiQue was reinforced the line.	
	29.		After having this line was evacuated and a position taken up the Reverse slope of the high ground N. of TRESLON. The enemy attacked this ridge in the afternoon but were repulsed	

WAR DIARY
or
INTELLIGENCE SUMMARY.
(Erase heading not required.)

Army Form C. 21

Place	Date	Hour	Summary of Events and Information	Remarks and references to Appendices
	29		Sunrise. The enemy following the early attack by a counter attack and there were heavy troops advancing, the effort was now check again. The French on the Rgt Lt were then forced back and a withdrawal to the BOULEUSE Ridge was made. This at once came very severe, but many Rgt forward were attacked by the enemy. After a sharp fight we remained in possession of the crest.	
	30.		At about 12 P.M. a counter advance was made to the high ground East of SARCY in the neighbourhood of LE SARCY-BOUILLY Road, this crest was already held by the French. In the evening the Bn retired to relieve a detachm of Shropshire Lt Infantry (19 Division) and dug in on the Sunken Road West of BLIGNY. Col. H. Baring was wounded here. Casualties in period 27th — 31st May.	
			O.R.s 7 Killed 70 O.Rs wounded 536 — Missing	
			1 Officer Killed 14 wounded 15 Missing	

W.H. Stevens Capt & Comdg
7th R Welch

WAR DIARY
INTELLIGENCE SUMMARY

1/Worcestershire R. Ref Map CHALONS. ABBEVILLE

H2W
8 June

Place	Date	Hour	Summary of Events and Information	Remarks
June	17/5		The Bn in line consisting of 3 O/Rs and 700 O.Rs formed into 1st & 2nd Composite Bns. Bn. furnished in western edge of BOIS DE COURTON. T'port at BERGERES. 10 O/Rs joined Bn.	
	8/6		T'port moved to PETIT BROUSSY	
	9/10		Billeted in PETIT BROUSSY.	
	11.		1/5th Composite Bn relieved in line	
	12		Hqrs of 1/8th Composite Bn joined Newsport.	
	13.		Moved by Horse Route to SEZANNE entrained and detrained at PONT REMY at 5PM on 14th June. Marched to billets in HUPPY	
			Billeted in HUPPY.	
	15/16		as above	
	17.		Sent out 70 Ro to 1 ents WO, DSO, MC joined the Bn.	
	18.		as above. 10 O/Rs to 1 DO O/Rs joined the Bn.	
	19		as above. 2 O/Rs + 226 + joined the Bn. 100 O/Rs joined the Bn	
	20		y.O.C. put Bn in inspection the Bn	
	21.		Billeted in HUPPY. 2 O/Rs + 114 O/Rs joined Bn.	
	22.		Marched at 6am to billets in DARGNIES.	

Army Form C. 2118.

WAR DIARY
or
INTELLIGENCE SUMMARY.
(Erase heading not required.)

Instructions regarding War Diaries and Intelligence Summaries are contained in F. S. Regs., Part II. and the Staff Manual respectively. Title pages will be prepared in manuscript.

Place	Date	Hour	Summary of Events and Information	Remarks and references to Appendices
June	23/25		Billeted in DARGNIES. Reorganised and commenced training, drill when detarm commanders.	
	26		As above. 50 NCOs & 530 ORs joined.	
	27	30	As above. Training continued. Artillery formation and Attacks. 10 hr attached.	

W.C. Stevens Capt Adjut
1/Worc R

D.A.G. G.H.Q.
3rd Echelon

Herewith War Diary
for July 1918.

1/8/1918.

L Smith 2Lt A/Adjt
for LIEUT. COL
COMDG. 1ST BN THE WORCESTERSHIRE REGT.

1st Bn. The Worcestshire Regt. WAR DIARY

Jun 1. 1918.   Worcester Rgt.   Vol 4

Army Form C. 2118.

INTELLIGENCE SUMMARY.

(Erase heading not required.)

Place	Date	Hour	Summary of Events and Information	Remarks and references to Appendices
DAOURS	1st		Battn in Training	
	2nd		" "	
	3rd		" "	
	4th		Battn moved by march route to camp at ONIVAL — Weather fair — Distance 9 miles	
ONIVAL	5th		Battn in Training. Weather Good. 1st Bn Bank formed Old Gang Members	
	6th		" "	
	7th		Divine Service	
	8th		Battn in Training - A cross country run, was held in the afternoon	
	9th		Battn in Training.	
	10th		" " Battn Sports day Sports were spoilt by continual rain 1 Off. panned	

Army Form C. 2118.

WAR DIARY
INTELLIGENCE SUMMARY.
(Erase heading not required.)

Instructions regarding War Diaries and Intelligence Summaries are contained in F. S. Regs., Part II. and the Staff Manual respectively. Title pages will be prepared in manuscript.

Place	Date	Hour	Summary of Events and Information	Remarks and references to Appendices
ONIVA	11		Batn. training. Weather wet.	
	12		RAIN.	
	13		Brigade Scheme. Weather fair 2 off. 40. O/Rs tonne	
	14		Divine Service	
	15		Bn. moved to DARGNIES. Weather Good.	
DARGNIES	16		Batn. training	
	17		do	
	18		do	
	19		do and preparation for move.	
	20		Marched to WOINCOURT STN. entrained at 9am. Detrained at AUBIGNY and marched to CAMBLAIN L'ABBÉ. weather fair	

Army Form C. 2118.

WAR DIARY
INTELLIGENCE SUMMARY.
(Erase heading not required.)

Instructions regarding War Diaries and Intelligence Summaries are contained in F.S. Regs., Part II. and the Staff Manual respectively. Title pages will be prepared in manuscript.

Place	Date	Hour	Summary of Events and Information	Remarks and references to Appendices
CAMBLAIN L'ABBE	21st		Divine Service	
	22nd		Entrained at 11.30 am for line relieved 1/4th K.O.S.B. in support at PETIT VIMY.	
PETIT VIMY	23rd		Working Parties Weather fair	
	24th		do — do —	
	25th		do — do —	
	26th		do — do —	
	27th		do — weather wet	
	28th		do — 1 O. Rank wounded	
	29th		do — Relieved 2nd N.N. Regt in line (MERICOURT SECTOR)	
	30th		During the morning	
TRENCHES	3rd		Weather good	P. Smith 2nd D/Sgt 1/ More Rgt

WAR DIARY

Rg Rlgt HAROEUL Army Form C. 2118.
1/Worcestershire R.

INTELLIGENCE SUMMARY.
(Erase heading not required.)

Place	Date	Hour	Summary of Events and Information	Remarks and references to Appendices
Aug	1st.		Bn in Trenches HERICOURT Sector. Attack of Enemy quiet. Enemy carried out shelling attacks Coy relief. 7 O/Rs 31 O/Rs wounded.	
	2.		Active Enemy aeroplane brought down by L/G fire. 6 O/Rs found.	
	3/6		As above. Weather good	
	7.		Relieved during the morning by the 1/Sherwood Foresters. Entrained at LATARGETTE from Roens and proceeded to DURHAM'S LANCASTER Camp Mont St ELOY. 10hr 7 O/Rs joined.	
	8.		Camp day devoted to General cleaning up. HQs Major & Bn marched through Mont St ELOY in red afternoon Bn the Routes.	
	9.		Day devoted to reorganisation inspections 4 O/Rs 25 O/Rs joined. 5 O/Rs 4 O/Rs joined.	
	10.		Day devoted to drill Gas drills & Sports. 1 O/R joined.	
	11.		Divine Services Schemes on the Training joined at VICTRIA An	
	12		Platoon Section BOIS.	
	13/15		Bn Training Special attention paid to ta Training of Sections and free movement. 2 O/Rs 3 O/Rs joined. 3 O/Rs cmn 3 O/Rs joined	5 sheet
	16.		Bn enjoyed of GPL and relieved the 6th Hgtld cunf dept Infantry in the OPPY Sector. Relief completed 19/30 pm Sector View (9 cull).	

WAR DIARY or INTELLIGENCE SUMMARY

Army Form C. 2118.

Place	Date	Hour	Summary of Events and Information	Remarks and references to Appendices
August	17/10		In the line OPPY Sector. Work concentrated on the Main Line of Defence. Enemy very active. Quiet. Several reconnaissance patrols sent out but were unable to enter enemy line.	7 ORs joined
	22		Enemy very heavily bombarded the line with gas from 10pm to 4am causing 1 Offr & 16 ORs casualties.	1 Offr & 19 ORs joined
	23		Defence Scheme altered and necessitated the digging of a new trench between the Main ARLEUX Rd and TOMMY ALLEY. Work which was very heavy while gas concentration commenced. Another 1 ORs Killed, 2 ORs wounded causing 1 Offr & 10 ORs casualties. 1 OR joined. 1 OR wounded.	20 Offrs & 8 ORs wounded
	24		Trench completed and men resumed previous concentration.	
	25		Work of laying duck boards, resetting and wiring continued on new trench which was named "WORCESTERSHIRE Trench".	2 ORs wounded
	26		From Bde Two Coys were working on a scheme of Outposts where Orders were received to send out patrols and find out where the enemy was. After their patrols had gone orders received to establish ourselves in enemy's system. A Coy did this patrol and established themselves in ARLEUX LOOP SOUTH. D Coy then followed and found fort South. Very serious opposition was met in SEVERN ALLEY where a block was made. Our line was held.	

D.A.G.
3rd Echelon
Base

Herewith War Diary
for the month of September 1918.

L. Smith 2Lt
for LIEUT. COL.
COMDG. 1ST BN THE WORCESTERSHIRE REGT.

4/10/18

ORDERLY ROOM
4 OCT 1918
No. 13/1024
1ST BN. WORC. REGIMENT

WAR DIARY or INTELLIGENCE SUMMARY

Army Form C. 2118.

1 Worcesters
9/12 46

45W
3 sheet

Place	Date	Hour	Summary of Events and Information	Remarks and references to Appendices
Oppy Front	Sept 1st	—	Bn. in the line — Oppy sector	
"	" 2nd	—	weather fair — 2 ORs joined	
"	" 3rd	—	weather fair — 1 OR wounded, 1 OR wd (gas)	
"	" 4th	—	weather fair — 6 ORs joined — 6 ORs wounded (gas)	
"	" 5th	—	weather fair — 1 OR killed — 2 ORs wounded (gas)	
"	" 6th	—	weather good — 4 ORs joined — 2 ORs wounded (gas)	
"	" 7th	—	weather good — 19 ORs joined (gas)	
"	" 8th	—	weather good — 8 ORs wounded (gas)	
"	" 9th	—	weather wet — 20 ORs joined Bn.	
"	" 10th	—	weather wet — 4 ORs joined — 1 OR wd. (gas)	
"	" 11th	—	weather wet — 4 ORs joined — 10 ORs wd (gas)	
"	" 12th	—	weather wet — 5 ORs wounded — 1 OR killed	
"	" 13th	—	weather wet — 2 ORs wounded (gas)	
"	" 14th	—	weather wet — 2 ORs wounded (gas)	
"	" 15th	—	weather fair — 3 ORs joined — 1 OR wd (gas)	
"	" 16th	—	weather good — 1 OR wounded. Raid on hostile trenches	
"	" 17th	—		
"	" 18th	—	11 ORs joined	
"	" 19th	—		
"	" 20th	—	93 ORs joined	

WAR DIARY

INTELLIGENCE SUMMARY

Army Form C. 2118.

Place	Date	Hour	Summary of Events and Information	Remarks and references to Appendices
Oppy Front	Apr 21st 1917		Bn in the line Oppy sector — 1 O.R. joined — Night attack on hostile trenches — all objectives gained — 3 unwounded prisoners captured. 2 O.Rs wounded	
	" 22nd			
	" 23rd		Bn in the line OPPY sector — 3 O.Ranks wounded	
	" 24th			
	" 25th		— 4 O.Ranks joined	
	" 26th			
	" 27th			
	" 28th		— 4 O.Ranks joined	
	" 29th		Bn moved to CELLAR CAMP, NEUVILLE ST VAAST — march wet.	
	" 30th			

L Smith 2Lt
Adjt 1st Worc Regt.

SECRET

O.D.a.
GHQ

Herewith War Diary
of the Bn under my
command, for month of
June.

H.C.W.
LIEUT. COL.
COMDG. 1ST BN. THE WORCESTERSHIRE REGT.

1/7/19.8.

24th Bde. 8th Division

War Diary

1st Bn, Worcestershire Regt.

October 1918.

WAR DIARY or INTELLIGENCE SUMMARY

Army Form C. 2118.

1/Worcestershire Regt.
Ref. Sheet OPPY.

46 W
6 sheet

No 47

Place	Date	Hour	Summary of Events and Information	Remarks and references to Appendices
October	1/5		Bn in Line S. of OPPY on our right Front Line – CANNIBAL and CHEDDAR Trenches. Three Coys in Support along BOIS – TYNE ALLEY and MARINE Trenches. Enemy quiet. Work of improving communications was carried out and preparations made for an advance. 10th HORs turned Bn. 2 ORs wounded.	
	7.		A bout at the Junction of LINK and OPPY Support trenches handed over to us the previous night and at 5 a.m. B Coy then holding the Front Line carried out a very successful operation and cleared OPPY Support. Two platoons under 2nd Lieut [name] firing up along the Ref between CRUFT and CHALK attacked [enemy?] in a Northerly direction of this same time a mopping attack was carried out by the remainder of B Coy faring OPPY Support in a Southerly direction. The trench was completely cleared and yielded 21 M.G.s and 18 prisoners. On the completion of the operation B Coy was lined up along the trenches from [?] coord to the FRESNES-ROUVROY LINE In addition to trip wire was set up over C1 & C2.3, but this was over come and a connection made at this junction of LINK and the FRESNES ROUVROY Line. D Coy platoon then bombed to the North and got in touch with the Inniskillings. To others on our left. The remainder of D coy started to bombard Ku5, but a counter attack pushed them back to the Post W.0.21 to Ku.S. C Coy then took up the fighting [and?] pushed forward along E. Coy Front line after a hard [struggle?] as far as [?] as [?] ACORN. A party	

WAR DIARY or INTELLIGENCE SUMMARY

Army Form C.118.

Ref Sheet OPPY. 44d S.E.

(Erase heading not required.)

Instructions regarding War Diaries and Intelligence Summaries are contained in F.S. Regs., Part II. and the Staff Manual respectively. Title pages will be prepared in manuscript.

Place	Date	Hour	Summary of Events and Information	Remarks and references to Appendices
	8.		Troops south of the Bn Boundary but were could not be gained with the 2nd Bde on the Right. This operation yielded 11 MGs and 36 prisoners 2/Lts. 1 OR/10 1 OR Rs wounded 1 OR killed.	
	9.		CONSTABLE and CRANE occupied without opposition. 2 Northamptonshire Regt went through the Bn and continued the advance. The Bn withdrew to BLANFORD LINK and CHEDDAR.	
	10.		Work started on a Nulahack [?] line the BAILLEUL OPPY Road to the FRESNES ROUVROY LINE by one Coy the remainder of the Bn went forward again and occupied the FRESNES ROUVROY LINE each Coy having one (J.W.) Lewis Platoon in CONSTABLE. 2 ORs wounded.	
	11.		The Bn was lent to the 2/Northamptonshire Regt acting as advance guard to the Bde and moved forward and occupied the QUEANT-DROCOURT LINE from 12E 4 to CREST WOOD.	
	12.		Moved forward and occupied the Railway cutting from LA MOTTE to BEAUMONT. 6 ORs wounded.	
	13/4.	1400 hours	A Coy arrived forward and relieved the 2 Northamptonshire Regt who were occupying a position along the PLANQUES – CITE OUVRIERE Road. The village of FLERS was made good and the Roads leading eastwards became the Road running in to I.B.R in advance of the Coy to bring up a position along the	

WAR DIARY or INTELLIGENCE SUMMARY

Army Form C. 2118.

Ref Sheet 44A S.E.

Place	Date	Hour	Summary of Events and Information	Remarks and references to Appendices
	13/4		Main PLANQUES Road. Capt A.E Prosser commanding B Coy then went forward and had a personal reconnaissance of the ground as far East as the HAUTE DEULE CANAL. C.Coy then went forward and dug in along the CANAL bank through the wood. A Machine Gun was captured on the Rly embankment and 5 Mauritz on the E. bank of the Canal by Capt Prosser and a few another. Down however the enemy, who in an extremely heavy shell fire put before Barrage, that it was impossible to distinguish it and the enemy barrage. The ground came across the trying to the South and the N from AUBY and C. Coy severely ground, sustaining very severe casualties was forced to withdraw. HQ was established at W1 D 87 from carrying this out. A forward action was directed by Major WY Frankle D.S.O. which the operation was indeed and a direct hit was represented. FLERS was then heavily shelled and Bn HQ. 1 Offr Killed 2 " wounded 1 " wounded and missing 1 " missing 10 ORs killed 31 " wounded 50 " missing	
	15.		B Coy took over the piquet line in front of FLERS, the remainder of the Bn remained in the Rly cutting. The Bombardment of FLERS continued with great intensity. 2 ORs wounded.	

WAR DIARY Ref/Nut. A4 O.S.E. Army Form C. 2118.
or
INTELLIGENCE SUMMARY.
(Erase heading not required.)

Place	Date	Hour	Summary of Events and Information	Remarks and references to Appendices
	16.		The Picquet Nine East of FLERS was held and no further advance made. Major W. Trouth D.S.O. ordered no furn RECRUITS.	
	17.		The Authore of Enemy was noi quiet. Withdrawing and reconnaissance down to the Canal Bank were much of an Officer of B Coy who reported all clear. B Coy was sent forward to Canal with D Coy following. A Lt. F. Roberts & was across the Canal first pushed forward and occupied BERNICOURT Chateau Q.3.a. He then went forward to BAS LIEZ where he cleared the village of an enemy patrol numbering ten who many were in the b. The passage across the Canal was very difficult indeed. The only remained a broken girder bridge at Q.33.a.40.20. over which it was possible for one man to scramble at a time. B Coy croft by a pony load supplied by the Division on the Left. Capt R.A.O Dormer commanding B Coy went forward with one Platoon & occupied BERNICOURT CHATEAU. D Coy scrambled across the girder bridge one man at a time. The crossing was not complete till 5 P.M. In the meantime, the Pole Boundaries had been changed to include th' H.Q. remainder of B Coy and D Coy and took up a position along the Road running N & S through Q.35.b - D. (M. Rly running E & East and West and was our northern Boundary) ready for the advance the the following morning. The Remainder of the Bn. remained at FLERS.	

Army Form C. 2118.

Instructions regarding War Diaries and Intelligence Summaries are contained in F. S. Regs., Part II and the Staff Manual respectively. Title pages will be prepared in manuscript.

WAR DIARY or INTELLIGENCE SUMMARY.

(Erase heading not required.)

Place: Ref Sheet 44A S.E.

Date	Hour	Summary of Events and Information	Remarks and references to Appendices
48.		At 7am in a very thick mist the advance was resumed by D Coy. One platoon advancing as a screen the remaining three platoons following up in column along the Rly. Severe opposition was met along the Rly. W. of RACHES Int by a m.gun. RACHES was in our possession. Touch was maintained throughout the advance on the Left but touch could not be established on the Right. One platoon was pushed along the N. bank of the SCARPE canal on either side of the RACHES Road to act as a defensive flank. A Coy in the meantime had been ordered to be in support in position along the Rly Embankment just West of the junction of the RACHES along the Rly Embankment. One platoon was ordered forward to RACHES. With the Rly Embankment was in position on the SCARPE. The screen went forward again followed by the remaining two platoons of D Coy. Hard spot ANHIERS, ANCIENNE ABBEYE (R19.D) and MONTREUIL also the woods to the South. Such slight opposition. 1MG + 2 prisoners being captured by 2/Lieut Nicholls M.C. 40 of screen, who afterwards was unfortunately killed. A Coy occupied RACHES and relieved the platoon of D Coy along the canal bank which was sent forward to join D Coy. The line MONTREUIL and road to hi S. (R35.D) Rifles S.W. being head to X10 central — Canal was extended with Re Section H.G. in Turner 2 BERLINES, A Capt at RACHES (nearly to advance on the west (Low) B Coy in village up 2/3 and C Coy and C Coy and HQ SCSGNI) 10½ = 2 ORs killed.	

A.5834 Wt. W4973/M687 750,000 8/16 D. D. & L. Ltd. Forms/C.2118/13.

Army Form C. 2118.

WAR DIARY
or
INTELLIGENCE SUMMARY.
(Erase heading not required.)

Instructions regarding War Diaries and Intelligence Summaries are contained in F. S. Regs., Part II. and the Staff Manual respectively. Title pages will be prepared in manuscript.

Place	Date	Hour	Summary of Events and Information	Remarks and references to Appendices
	19.		The 1/Shrewsbury Foresters went through the Bn, which were concentrated and billeted in ANHIERS billets good.	
	20.		Bn remained at ANHIERS.	
	21.		Bn moved at 1 PM and billeted in BOUVIGNIES	
	22.		Remained at BOUVIGNIES. Day devoted to reorganisation and the making of temporary NCOs.	
	23.		Bn moved and billeted in HILLON FOSSE. Remained at HILLONFOSSE Day devoted to reorganisation of Coys into 4 sections.	
	24.		As above.	
	25.		Moved to LA CROISETTE and billeted in the HOTEL ST MICHAEL.	
	26.		Moved at 4 PM and billeted in hospital ST MAND	
	27.		Moved at 11 am to HILLONFOSSE	
	28.		Remained at HILLON FOSSE day devoted to general cleaning up and reorganisation of Coys into 4 sections.	
	29.		Moved at 9 am to MARCHIENNE billets fair.	
	30.		C.O's Conference at MARCHIENNE herein programme observed and particulars recieved on recent operations.	
	31.		The C.O.C. 1st Army and the Corps visited MARC HIENNES at 3 PM. Guard of Honour supplied by B Coy and one commanded by Capt R.A.Osborne 4C. Guard congratulated by the Army and Corps Commanders on Turn out and steadiness of men. (Sgd) G.W. [?] Capt & Adjt	

WAR DIARY or INTELLIGENCE SUMMARY

1/Worcestershire Regt.
Ref Sheet VALENCIENNES.

Vol 48

Place	Date	Hour	Summary of Events and Information	Remarks and references to Appendices
Marchura	1/4		Battalion billeted in HARCHIENNES carried out schemes in open warfare. Inspected by S.C. of Div. Special attention paid to	9 ORs joined
	5		Battalion inspected by S.C. of Div. Special attention paid to Battalion Organisation after Infantry Fire and form mt. Tan S.M.	3 ORs
	6		O.B.1919 Organisation. The C.O. on the parade on at 9.30 the Bn was informed congratulated the C.O. on the parade and said that the Bn was informed Billets in Marchiennes – Route March – Inspecting Bde	20 ORs joined 2 ORs —
	7		Coules Bn were quarters out of 400. — Route March —	
	8		As above – Brigade Concert.	
	9		(a) Lebrun – Brigade Concert. Moved from 0730 hrs by Route Marche and billeted at the Hotel Thurine LACROISETTE location (my orders army HQ) The B.O. at CUGEX retreats VQ DIOMC Estimate Jour 8 at FRANCE-le-ineraz	8 ORs joined
	10		Moved from LACROISETTE 0910 hrs by march Route thus billeted at BERNISSART were thus excel. Billets good	
	11		Billets in BERNISSART. Hostilities were as usual played in square. Among the civil population. Band played in square. HARCHIES.	
	12		Moved at 0945 hrs by uncovered route and billeted in HARCHIES weather and roads good.	7 ORs joined
	13/15		Billeted in HARCHIES. Several much lening up parades on 15th. Transport moved by march Route to HERGNIES.	4 pm Relief

1/Worcestershire Regt.
Ref sheet
TOURNAI

Army Form C. 2118.

WAR DIARY
or
INTELLIGENCE SUMMARY.
(Erase heading not required.)

Place	Date	Hour	Summary of Events and Information	Remarks and references to Appendices
November	16.		Moved by Rail Route and billeted in TOURNAI weather cold. Wet & very great.	
	17/30		Billeted in TOURNAI. Time Devoted to Reverent Cleaning, managing up Rev Ceremonial Parades + Route Marches. Educational Training taken from 1100 – 12.30 hrs daily – about 200 Candidates.	
			17 Nov. L. offr's 4 O.Rs joined	
			20 " " 1 O.R. " 7	
			22 " 1 " 6	
			24 " 1 " 3	
			25 " 1 " 3 Canadian	
			27 " 1 " 94 Draft.	
			29 " " 6	

1st Review Copy. O.C. D/A Ctt
1/Worct

Jan - Apl 1919

D.A.G.
3rd Echelon

Herewith War Diary
for January 1919.

W.V. Franklin
LIEUT. COL.
COMDG. 1ST BN THE WORCESTERSHIRE REGT.

3/2/1919

WAR DIARY or **INTELLIGENCE SUMMARY**

1/Worcestershire Regt Ref Sheet TOURNAI 5.

Army Form C. 2118.

Place	Date	Hour	Summary of Events and Information	Remarks and references to Appendices
December	1.		Bn billeted in TOURNAI. Supplied guard to III Corps Commander.	
	2.		Colour party as usual proceeded to WORCESTER to receive the Colours from the Dean at the Cathedral.	
			Capt W.C. Shewan MC 2 rans Croix de Guerre.	
			2/Lt Esh worked	
			A/RSM G Cundip HC Dcm, rBar Croix de Guerre.	
			C.H.E. Frazier DCM, Bar.	
			H Rowlands DCM. MM.	
	3/4.		Devoted to Educational & Recreational Training.	
	5.		Ceremonial Parade at 11.30 hrs The O.C. on driving billeted TOURNAI and distributed medals.	
	6.		Diol. Boxing Tournament. Exhibit weight won by the Battalion.	
	7.		His Majesty King GEORGE visited TOURNAI general of honour supplied by the Bn.	
	8/10		Educational and Recreational Training.	
	11.		Bn received Rgt medal Colour. Ceremonial Parade in the PLACE DU PARC TOURNAI.	
	12/16		Billeted in TOURNAI. Time devoted to Educational Recreational Training.	
	17.		Bn moved to LEUZE by Route march. weather good.	
	18.		Moved by March Route from LEUZE to HESLIN LEVEQUE. Roads bad and weather wet.	

48 W
2 sheets

Army Form C. 2118.

WAR DIARY
or
INTELLIGENCE SUMMARY.

(Erase heading not required.)

Place	Date	Hour	Summary of Events and Information	Remarks and references to Appendices
December	19.		Billeting & reorganisation to meet that Dcoy was moved to LANGUESAINT.	
	20.		General reorganisation of Billeting Area and settling down.	
	21.		The O.C. & 2nd i/c Dium are Brigadier Comdg. 24 in Inf. Bde inspected Billets	
	22/31.		Bn. Located in HESDIN & VERQUIN. Time devoted to Recreational and Educational Training. Due football (Association) League started also an Association League games Rugger. Boxing competitions for put.	

W C Stevens Capt
A/Adjt 1 Worc R.

WAR DIARY
INTELLIGENCE SUMMARY
(Erase heading not required.)

1/Worcestershire Regt. Army Form C.
Ref. See Journal 3.

Place	Date	Hour	Summary of Events and Information	Remarks Appendices
January	3.		During the whole month the Bn has been Billeted at MESNIL L'EVEQUE. The mornings have been devoted to physical Training, infantry and company education and Military training. The afternoons have been devoted to recreational training. An inter platoon football competition has been played throughout the month. The Battalion team has played continuously in the Divl Football League. A Battalion concert party was inaugurated early in the month which gave concerts every week. The weather throughout the month has been very bad, the first part very wet, and the latter part a continual frost, with down falls of snow which has interfered to a certain extent the recreational training.	
	14/15.		Bde Boxing Tournament held at SILLY. The Battalion won two weights.	
	18		Lt Col J C ROBB VC DSO MC left for England.	
	28		Lt Col W FRANKLIN DSO rejoined the Bn from leave in England.	
	30/31.		8th Divl Novices Boxing Tournament held at ENGHIEN. Bn had two Runners up in the Finals.	

W C Mears Capt
1/Worcestershire Regt.

WAR DIARY
INTELLIGENCE SUMMARY
(Erase heading not required.)

Army Form C. 2118.

1/Worcestershire Regt. Sheet Tournai 2/8 51

Place	Date	Hour	Summary of Events and Information	Remarks and references to Appendices
February	1/9		Battalion billeted in MESLIN L'EVÊQUE. During this period it was impossible to carry out very extensively Recreational Training owing to deep falls of snow and extremely hard frost.	
	10		Battalion moved by march route to ATH where it was accommodated in the Infantry Barracks.	
	11/28		Battalion billeted in ATH. Time devoted to Recreational and Educational Training. Football was played with great success against the 2nd Brigade. On the 20th Feb a draft of 100 ORs & 2/Lt ORs was sent to join the 2/8 Worcestershire Regt at CHERBOURG, the men requiring exchanges of uniform to supply 100 ORs. The Battalion was beaten in the semi-final of the Divisional Football League by the 9th Divl Ammunition Column.	

W C Stewart Capt
1/Worcestershire Regt.

50 W
1 sheet

SECRET

D.A.G.
3rd Echelon

Herewith War Diary
March 1919.

F. D. Baker Capt.,
for LIEUT. COL.

Army Form C. 2118.

WAR DIARY
or
INTELLIGENCE SUMMARY.
(Erase heading not required.)

Instructions regarding War Diaries and Intelligence Summaries are contained in F. S. Regs., Part II. and the Staff Manual respectively. Title pages will be prepared in manuscript.

Vol 52

Place	Date	Hour	Summary of Events and Information	Remarks and references to Appendices
ATH (BELGIUM)	1st to 31st March 1919		The Bn. was billeted in ATH. The strength of the Bn. which was 26 Officers and 1147 O.R.s on the 1st, was reduced to 116 [?] - 538 O.R.s by the end of the month, 3 of the officers, 10 who actually reporting with the Bn.	
ATH	3rd March		The 14th Bde. reduced to Cadre strength and was merged into 73rd Bde, both Bdes. were then commanded by Brig. General G.W. St.G. Grogan V.C., C.M.G., D.S.O.	
ATH	13th March		The Divisional Commander said good-bye at the H.Q. 23rd Bde. to the officers of the Division and left the Division next day.	
ATH	31-3-19		There has been little effort during the month and most it is almost entirely out the personnel of the Bn. being employed.	

P.D. Baker Capt.
1st Norf.

April 1919
1/Worcestershire Reg^t

WAR DIARY
or
INTELLIGENCE SUMMARY. Ref Sheet TOURNAI 5.

Army Form C. 2118.

Place	Date	Hour	Summary of Events and Information	Remarks and references to Appendices
	1/11.		Battalion billeted in ATH	
	12.		The 4th Bn Worcestershire Reg^t arrived from the vicinity of COLOGNE and took over Mobilization Stores and equipment of Battalion.	
	13.		Received warning orders to entrain on Wednesday the 16th instant. General preparations for the move.	
	14/15/16.		The Cadre entrained at ATH & train left at 17.45 hrs. The Band of the 4th Bn Worcesters and Drums of the 4th Bn played the Cadre to the Station. Continuous cheers were played at the Station by all the Ranks of the remaining Units of the Division. A very big crowd of Belgian and Civilians watched the departure of the Cadre.	
	17.		Arrived DUNKIRK at 13.30 hrs. The men were given eleven of A Camp. The Afternoon was devoted to Bathing and delousing after which the Cadre moved to No.2 Camp where the remained for the night.	
	18.		Day devoted to adjusting of Papers required by Camp and Embarkation Authorities. "Nancy" the Regimental Pet was examined and found free from Foot & Mouth disease.	
	19.		Cadre moved away from No.2 Camp at 09.45 hrs and embarked on the S.S. "ANTRIM at Monitor Quai at 11.00 hrs and set sail at 12.00 hrs the passage was a very smooth one and the Band of the 2nd Northamptonshire Reg^t played on deck	52W 2 cheer

Army Form C. 2118.

WAR DIARY
or
INTELLIGENCE SUMMARY.

(Erase heading not required.)

Instructions regarding War Diaries and Intelligence Summaries are contained in F. S. Regs., Part II. and the Staff Manual respectively. Title pages will be prepared in manuscript.

Place	Date	Hour	Summary of Events and Information	Remarks and references to Appendices
	20.		Arrived at DOVER at 15.00 hrs. Much to the regret of the Battalion, the Customs Authorities prohibited the landing of Nancy the Regtl Mascot - she had to be abandoned and left on board the S.S. ANTRIM. The Bn had been through the SOMME and AISNE retirements. The men were given a meal at Dover also hard rations and entrained. The train leaving at 19.40 hrs. Victoria was reached at 20.00 hrs. The train from PADDINGTON to CHISLETON at 21.15 hrs could not be caught owing to the non arrival of the Motor Transport at Victoria. Entrained at PADDINGTON at 00.15 hrs. arrived at SWINDON at 02.30 hrs. Representatives of the 1st Battalion Foreign Service Details met us at SWINDON. Lorries conveyed the Coldre to CHISLEDON.	

W Skeens Capt & Adjt
1/Wore R

Place	Date	Hour	Summary of Events and Information	Remarks and references to Appendices
	26.		B. Coy then went in further South via MACHINE GUN Trench and TOMMY ALLEY and established themselves in TOMMY ALLEY. Bombed up Z Trench and TOMMY Trench but could only get down half way up there where they were formed and positions held on to. A Coy Patrol Parties were ordered to occupy Bo.Trench and support withdrawn (A.C.Coys ordered to occupy Bo.Trench and support respectively. 10/ORs wounded 10Rs killed 20Rs gassed casualties.	
	27.		During the morning the whole of ARLEUX LOOP SOUTH and Z Trench made from Owen's were received to hand on Z Trench at its value were free slipping to its South. Then at its value and ordered back to Bo.Support C Coy ordered D Coy relieved and ordered back to Bo.Support C Coy ordered forward to Bo.Trench and A Coy received forward lines up in HARQUI'S Trench and ordered to Carry ammunition attacks objectives whole hyphen on Bn front. This was carried out and made whilst the Sonies with all serious opposition. The enemy had tried from hours to bring in counter from BAT AL BERT but our position held casualties — 1 OR killed 11 ORs wounded 1 OR gassed.	
	28.		All Positions maintained. Two Platoons of C Coy sent up as support remainder of Coy relieved B Coy. 1 OR/s wounded.	

Army Form C. 2118.

WAR DIARY
or
INTELLIGENCE SUMMARY.
(Erase heading not required.)

Place	Date	Hour	Summary of Events and Information	Remarks and references to Appendices
	29.		Enemy counter attacked right flank and tried to come down Trench from OPPY POST he was prevented and numerous casualties inflicted At 1.45 some time he left flank was attacked but with no result. to the enemy	
	30.		Lt Col Te Rangi VC DSO MC and HQ of 2nd Franklin Bn reported Later Bn relief	
	31.		Right flank attacked but no result.	

WC Stevens Capt
A/Adjt 1 W of R

WAR DIARY
or
INTELLIGENCE SUMMARY.

(Erase heading not required.)

Army Form C. 2118.

Hour, Date, Place	Summary of Events and Information	Remarks and references to Appendices
Feb 12.	Fort Adieu. The latter of very large size inflicting with deafening noise, and making craters at least 15 to 18 feet in diameter. In consequence of this it became necessary to leave I.21.2 if men. Our howitzer retaliated in the course of the afternoon but did not inflict, so far as is known. I.15.2 wooden scarred heavily shelled in the course of the afternoon.	
Feb 13.	The enemy was seen more noisy today than yesterday, I.21.2 being heavily pounded with 5 shells, and several "whiz-bangs". Our artillery replied, and our 6" howitzers came into action, bombarding German trenches with good effect. I.21.2 was so knocked about	

WAR DIARY
or
INTELLIGENCE SUMMARY.
(Erase heading not required.)

Army Form C. 2118.

Hour, Date, Place	Summary of Events and Information	Remarks and references to Appendices
Feb 13	The whole Battalion was brought straight from Bois Grenier lines, to reinforce Indian Corps the enemy Int having broken through a big line X 15.2 we were also heavily shelled during the course of the afternoon. About 1.30 p.m. the company of the 2/6th Northumberland Fusiliers which were in the trenches on the our under instructions withdrew to billets. Trench H.Q was shelled about 12.30 pm and a Dug Out knocked in. A line F. sent in to the trenches to take their position.	
Feb 14	A quiet day in trenches, and advantage was taken of this to effect damaged parapets for about	

WAR DIARY
or
INTELLIGENCE SUMMARY.

(Erase heading not required.)

Army Form C. 2118.

Hour, Date, Place	Summary of Events and Information	Remarks and references to Appendices
Festubert	8.30 p.m we were relieved by 2.5/2 Northumberland Fusiliers (British Division) New Army. The relief firmly off very smoothly. The battalion going in billets was Jesus Farm, about 1½ miles from beginning. on North side of river Lys. the trenches were very bad to get out of trenches as the shelling on 12th and 13th had been pretty severe.	
15.	In above billets.	Very Windy
16.	In above billets	High Winds Fine
17.	In above billets. Working parties to Bois Grenier line Drainage billets.	Fine and Cold.
18.	In above billets. Preparing for move to Corps Reserve	Frosty & dull

Army Form C. 2118.

WAR DIARY
or
INTELLIGENCE SUMMARY.
(Erase heading not required.)

Instructions regarding War Diaries and Intelligence Summaries are contained in F. S. Regs., Part II. and the Staff Manual respectively. Title pages will be prepared in manuscript.

Hour, Date, Place	Summary of Events and Information	Remarks and references to Appendices
19	In above billets: drawing ground sand huts. Motor jackets	Draft & cell.
20	The Battalion left above billets for Vieux Berquin en route for Bufs Reserve. Heavy baggage had left the day previously in 3 motor lorries for Bufs advance area. Leading Company left Hulle 6 have been roads at 12 midnight strong. Remaining companies following at 10 minutes interval. Order of march A.B.C.D. Hulle 6 Roads taken Steenwerck — Vieux Berquin. Length of march about 10 miles. Battalion arrived in billets about 4 p.m. A few German aeroplanes flew very low over battalion about 12.50 p.m. between Hulle 6 between and Steenwerck.	After mid day Ideal for marching
21.	At 8.20 a.m. the Battalion broke up their billets near La Bourrasse about 1 mile South of Vieux Berquin church and marched forward to Bufs Reserve Area near Sercus. Order of march 1/Sherwoods. 2/E. Lancs. 1/Warws. 2/Manchesters.	

(73989) W4141—463. 400,000. 9/14. H.&J.Ltd. Forms/C. 2118/10.

Army Form C. 2118.

WAR DIARY
or
INTELLIGENCE SUMMARY.
(Erase heading not required.)

Instructions regarding War Diaries and Intelligence Summaries are contained in F.S. Regs., Part II. and the Staff Manual respectively. Title pages will be prepared in manuscript.

Hour, Date, Place	Summary of Events and Information	Remarks and references to Appendices
21	Route: Vieux Berquin; La Motte; Morbecque; Steenbecque; La Belle Hôtesse. About 11 a.m. Battalion arrived in new billets and were then distributed B & D Companies in cheese factory at Moulin Fontaine; A Company in second farm east of factory; C company in farms North of factory. HQ operating about 100 yards west of La Belle Hôtesse cross roads. The billets are on the M.L.R. was fair. Heavy baggage fetched up from Army heavy foot and sent to the head Q dump from them in the Basse [illegible]	A fine mild day. Much discipline on the whole was satisfactory considering the long hours Battalion had been in trenches.
22.	In above billets. Morning of [illegible]	Rather [illegible]
23.	In above billets. Orders received to proceed on 24th to Estaires about 7.30 p.m. Subsequently cancelled at 3.30 p.m.	Cold and snow all day. Cold and still snowing.

WAR DIARY
or
INTELLIGENCE SUMMARY.
(Erase heading not required.)

Army Form C. 2118.

Instructions regarding War Diaries and Intelligence Summaries are contained in F.S. Regs., Part II. and the Staff Manual respectively. Title pages will be prepared in manuscript.

Hour, Date, Place	Summary of Events and Information	Remarks and references to Appendices
24.	In above billets. Training.	Fair with N.E. wind
25.	In above billets. Training.	N.E. winds, Snow.
26.	In above billets. Route March.	Finer
27.	In above billets. Church Parade.	Cold
28.	In above billets. Orders received to move to BRUAY on 29/2.	
29.	At N. 9.20 a.m. battalion marched from billets, entraining at THIENNES at 11.30 p.m. Proceeded by train to CALONNE-RIACOURT where Bn. detrained at 1.p.m. Thence by march route 5 miles to BRUAY when they got into billets at about 5 p.m. Considerable delay was experienced after arrival in BRUAY before battalion was billeted, as the move being so urgent one, little preliminary arrangements were made. No British troops had been previously billeted in BRUAY in we relieved the French there. The billets were pretty good, and the attitude of inhabitants very friendly. Baggage did not arrive by road march convoys in billets till 1 a.m.	

Signed. M. Colonel
Comdg. 1st Oxford & Bucks Light Infantry Regt.